HIGH
ABOVE
LONDON

D&C
David and Charles

HIGH ABOVE LONDON

CONTENTS

Text
Barbara Roveda

Photographs
Jason Hawkes and
Nathan McConnel

Editorial coordination
Laura Accomazzo

Graphic Design
Marinella Debernardi

A DAVID & CHARLES BOOK
F&W Media International LTD 2011

David & Charles is an imprint of F&W Media International LTD,
Brunel House, Forde Close, Newton Abbot, TQ12 4PU, UK

F&W Media International, LTD is a subsidiary of F+W Media, Inc.,
4700 East Galbraith Road, Cincinnati OH45236, USA

© White Star Publishers,
Via Candido Sassone, 24
13100 Vercelli, Italia
www.whitestar.it

First published in the UK in 2011

ISBN-13: 978-1-4463-0151-7
ISBN-10: 1-4463-0151-6

Printed in China for:
F&W Media International, LTD
Brunel House, Forde Close, Newton Abbot, TQ12 4PU, UK

10 9 8 7 6 5 4 3 2 1

F+W Media publishes high quality books on a wide range of subjects
For more great book ideas visit www.rubooks.co.uk

1 Tower Bridge is the symbol of London and a splendid example of Victorian architecture.

2-3 The City, built on the ancient Roman settlement of Londinium, is the business center of the capital.

4-5 Buckingham Palace is the royal residence and stands at the center of a large green area.

6-7 The National Gallery is one of the world's leading art galleries, with over 2,000 paintings.

8 Big Ben is the name of the great bell housed in the clock tower of Westminster Palace. It is named after Benjamin Hall, who commissioned the works in 1858, the year in which the bell was inaugurated

9 This picture shows a rendering of the Aquatics Center, one of the buildings in the new Olympic Park.

10-11 Hyde Park is the oldest of the royal parks and was opened to the public at the beginning of

the seventeenth century by James I together with its extension, Kensington Gardens. It is one of the City's most important green areas, also because of its central position.

Introduction

An aerial view reveals the very essence of London. The largest and most populated metropolis in Europe is actually a collection of little villages that grew up around the original nucleus of the Roman town of Londinium. This disorderly urban sprawl, bounded by the ring of freeways that surrounds the City and bisected by the winding course of the Thames, is interrupted only by the sporadic green areas of the parks and gardens of which the City is so proud. These villages have developed over the course of many years and are not simply geographical districts, for each has its own history, character and, even, rhythm, which are illustrated in the splendid photographs by Jason Hawkes and Nathan McConnel

The City of London, which is practically a separate, autonomously governed body from the 32 boroughs that comprise Greater London; together they cover an area of almost 620 square miles. Inner London is constituted by the 12 boroughs closest to the City, while the remaining 20 form what is known as Outer London. However, complex administrative divisions aside, it is the sheer diversity of the districts' architecture, landscapes and lifestyles of their inhabitants that distinguishes them, to the point that many people indicate their quarter of residence, as in the case of Richmond, rather than London as their home City.

An aerial viewpoint thus clearly shows that London is not one, but many cities grouped together. There are the modern skyscrapers of the City and the stately and spectacular palaces of Westminster, which testify to the City's regal magnificence. It is home to both monuments that have become authentic icons, known and recognized worldwide as the City's distinctive landmarks—Big Ben, Westminster Abbey and Buckingham Palace—and the narrow streets of the City, hidden from the view of visitors.

The curious administrative structure of this part of London that covers just one square mile (it is independent of the Crown and Westminster and still organized in guilds that elect the Lord Mayor—the mayor of the City alone—each year) represents an almost archaic world, in contrast with the rapid modern pace that animates it. Indeed, each day it is frequented by around 500,000 white-collar workers and its offices are the setting for some of the most important transactions of the financial world.

Beyond the boundaries of the City, the elegant Georgian houses of the West End mark yet another London. The West End is both a residential district and a center of entertainment and has always been one of the richest areas of the City. Visitors can enjoy the tranquil atmosphere of the streets and airy squares of aristocratic Mayfair or descend on bustling Soho and Covent Garden to explore the fashionable stores and locales and let themselves be enchanted by acrobats and street artists. Alternatively, they can give themselves up to culture in neighboring Bloomsbury, which boasts one of the world's important museums—the British Museum—or let themselves be overwhelmed by the barrage of neon lights and cheap shops in chaotic Piccadilly Circus and Trafalgar Square.

After leaving the West End, visitors can delight in the art and trendy locales of the East End, witnessing how London never stands still. Once a working-class ghetto, this area has now become a focus of interest due to its up-and-coming quarters. Newly arrived communities of artists have mingled with those of exotic immigrants in Spitalfields and Whitechapel. The result is a bubbly blend of vitality, culture and entertainment, which has transformed these once shady districts into alternative tourist spots.

The City's latest great architectural revolution was worked on occasion of the Millennium celebra-

---

12-13 Pedestrian Leicester Square, enclosed between Trafalgar Square and Piccadilly Circus, is one of the principal squares of the West End, London's cinema and theater district. It is overlooked by four of the City's main cinemas, including that with the largest screen and that with the greatest seating capacity (over 2,000).

15 The Palace of Westminster is the official name of the Houses of Parliament and stands on the site of the old palace built by Edward the Confessor. It was designed by the Victorian architect Charles Barry between 1840 and 1888 in Neo-Gothic style as a tribute to nearby Westminster Abbey. Its Victoria Tower (foreground) is the largest and tallest square tower in the world and houses over one and a half million acts of Parliament dating back to 1497.

tions. The recent town planning experiments by the big names of architecture in the Docklands and on the South Bank have not only changed the City's skyline, but also its lifestyle. The historic district has thus been joined by an area that is almost a second City center, which differs from the former in both content and form. Museums and new locales have replaced the old factories in what was, until recently, a desolate area, neglected not only by tourists but by Londoners too. A good example is the Tate Modern, the section of the famous Tate Gallery dedicated to contemporary and modern art, housed in a former power station. The gigantic London Eye, on the other hand, is the largest ferris wheel in the world, while the old warehouses of the Docks have been converted into luxurious lofts inhabited by professionals and creative types.

Away from the center, the villages that make up Greater London are more easily recognized. The circular M25 freeway marks the City boundaries, but it is not necessary to cross it to find a landscape very different from that of the center. This is a separate world, where anonymous or enchanting suburbs recall individual villages, almost as though the City were many miles away. Hampstead, Richmond and Greenwich appear as satellites of the City, very well connected to it yet distant enough to have managed to escape industrialization and uncontrolled urbanization. These districts resemble small country towns, with narrow streets where life proceeds at a leisurely pace.

However, what makes London unique is its cultural variety, capable of combining old and modern culture and enhancing both to the fullest. The result is an evocative contrast, in terms of lifestyle as well as architecture. Ancient traditions and eccentricities still live on in Europe's most cutting-edge metropolis. The pubs continue to close when the night is still young on the rest of the continent, cars persist in driving on the "other" side of the road and the same taxis that could have been seen over 50 years ago still ply the streets. While on the subject of eccentricities, perhaps it should be noted that this is the only place in the world that could house a museum dedicated to a purely fictional character—the legendary Sherlock Holmes. However, this is also the City that gave rise to the punk movement and represents the first stop for all new trends—starting with music—that are not actually born here. London boasts more than one record with regard to lifestyle. It is the most exciting European City for shopping, comparable to a little New York in terms of sheer variety of choice: it is possible to find absolutely everything, from the street markets like Portobello and stores that look as though they haven't changed for a century to the most refined new designs, as well as objects and specialties from all over the world. The City has one of the most varied concert and theatre seasons in Europe and the best choice of musicals. In recent years London has even made a name for itself in the culinary field, dispelling the terrible reputation of English cooking and becoming a gourmet capital, also due to the presence of an incredible variety of cuisines from all over the world and its ability to create exceptionally high-quality fusion food. London is all of this and an aerial view offers a privileged vantage point for understanding this City of contrasts with a multicultural vocation, the most multi-ethnic European City. Each day its 70 square miles of greenery, 17,000 historic buildings, 200 museums and over 100 theaters are shared by its 7,000,000 inhabitants, belonging to 30 ethnic groups and speaking 300 different languages, who have always made London one of the world's liveliest cities.

16 Piccadilly Circus is one of London's most famous squares. It is dominated by an aluminum monument dedicated to the Duke of Shaftsbury that is popularly known as Eros, although it actually represents the Christian angel of Charity.

18-19 Bloomsbury has always been London's intellectual district. It is home to some of the City's leading academic and cultural institutes, including University College, the Royal Academy of Dramatic Art and the British Museum.

20-21 The British Museum is the country's largest museum and one of the most important in the world. It was founded in 1753 to gather historical testimony of all cultures, according to the posthumous wishes of the physician Hans Sloane. The stately neoclassical-style building occupies the entire block and has recently been extended with a glass dome, designed by British architect Norman Foster, that covers the huge internal Great Court.

22-23 The London Eye is the world's largest ferris wheel and was built for the Millennium

celebrations. It is composed of 30 glass cabins, which can carry up to 15,000 people a day. Its 450-foot summit offers views over the entire City and beyond on a clear day.

24-25 Each year over a million soccer and rugby supporters throng Wembley Stadium, which also hosts numerous concerts and international athletics events.

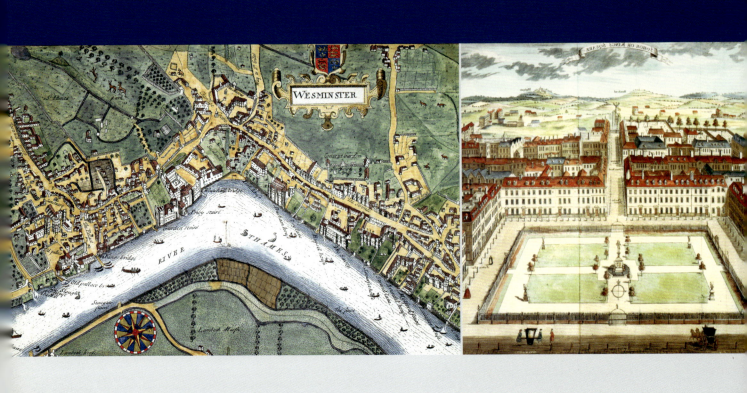

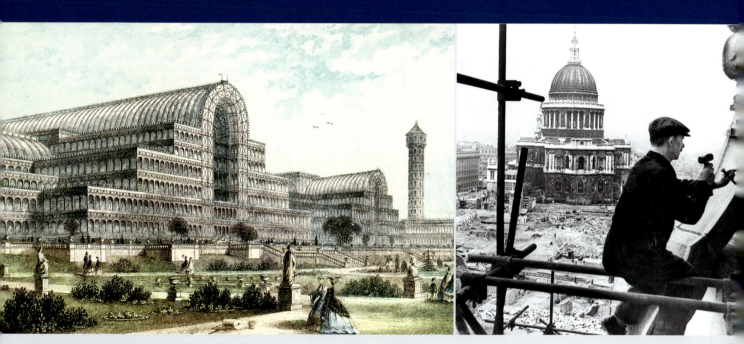

HISTORY

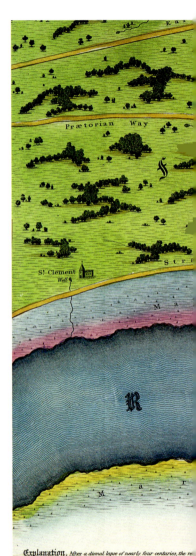

The history of London commences with a river and a group of wooden houses built on its banks. When the Romans arrived in the land of the Britons in 43 AD, Llyn-Din was just a small Celtic village and the Thames, which ran through marshy and insalubrious lands, chiefly an obstacle preventing further progress. The Roman troops were forced to build a bridge in order to cross it. There was little choice regarding its position: the first London Bridge was constructed at the narrowest point of the river, which was easily crossed and near enough to the sea to allow trade with the rest of the Empire. The first settlements appeared around this famous wooden bridge. In just two centuries the colony of Londinium became one of the most important Roman cities, a flourishing center of trade and an important strategic and military post. Its development was interrupted only briefly shortly after its foundation: not even 20 years had passed when Boudicca (or Boadicea), queen of the Iceni, challenged the conquerors to win back her crown. The Romans were victorious, but the village was burned to the ground and its inhabitants decimated.

Londinium was rebuilt and by 200 AD was a town of wooden houses gathered around various imposing Roman civic buildings. Its basilica was the largest west of the Alps and it also boasted a governor's palace, a forum, a fort, pagan temples and an amphitheater. A ring of defensive walls, 20 feet high and two miles around, was built. Although the walls no longer exist, ancient Londinium corresponds to the modern-day City of London, the financial heart of the City. The street known as London Wall follows part of the old course of the walls, the remains of which can still be seen between the Tower of London and Tower Hill, and the names of the old City gates are reflected in the local place names: Ludgate, Newgate, Bishopsgate and Aldgate. One of the most important Roman finds made in London was the Temple of Mithras, discovered near Walbrook and subsequently transferred to Queen Victoria Street, whereas several artifacts uncovered during the excavation are housed in the Museum of London. During the final years of the Empire, Londinium had a population of 45,000 and had become the capital of Maxima Caesariensis, one of the four Roman provinces of Britannia.

The City's decline commenced in the fourth century. The Roman Empire was devastated by the pillaging of the barbarian invaders, and in 410 AD Rome was forced to recall its troops to the European mainland, leaving Londinium undefended. This marked the start of a period of invasions by Germanic and Nordic peoples, and the City was dominated by an alternating succession of Saxons, Norwegians and Danes, attracted by its strategic position; however, these were also the years of Christianization. Towards the end of 596 Pope Gregory I sent Saint Augustine, the future Archbishop of Canterbury, to try to convert the English. The construction of St. Paul's Cathedral, one of London's most famous monuments also dates back to the same period. It was founded in 604, on what was probably a temple dedicated to Diana, and then rebuilt several times until reaching its present form.

During the years of Anglo-Saxon domination, Lundenwic, as it became known from 670, underwent great expansion and acquired new churches, streets and markets. In contemporary chronicles, the Venerable Bede, the greatest scholar of the Middle Ages, described it as "a trading place for many nations who visit it by land or sea". Great new changes ensued with the accession to the throne of the last Saxon king, Edward the Confessor, in 1042. His dream was to build the largest church in England; two miles west of the City he founded majestic Westminster Abbey (from "West Minister", the western church), which was to become the royal church, where almost all the English monarchs would be crowned and buried. London now had two centers: Westminster, the focus of political power, and the City, the heart of trade.

26-27 left to right
A plan of London in
1600; Soho Square
in a 1754
engraving; Crystal
Palace c.1850; a
workman restoring
the church of St.
Mary-Le-Bow
following bomb
damage suffered
during World
War II.

28 Edward the
Confessor, depicted
here during a
banquet, was the
last Saxon king,
crowned in 1042.
He was responsible
for the construction
of majestic
Westminster Abbey,
which was designed
to be the largest
church in England.

28-29 This color
lithograph of a
nineteenth-century
English school
shows a
reconstruction of the
plan of the City of
London at the time
of the Saxon
dynasty, around
1000 AD.

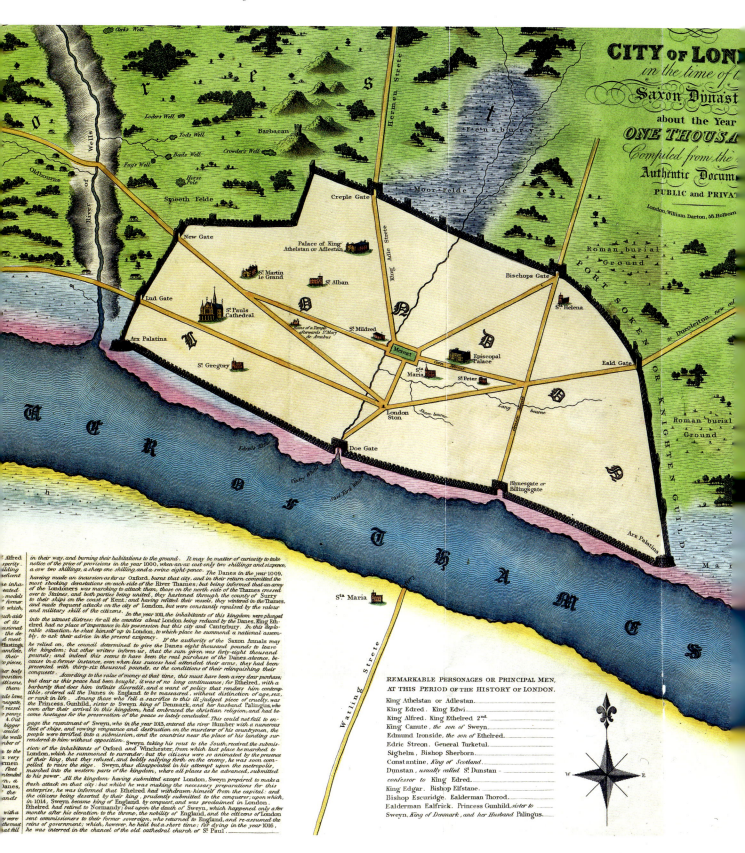

During the Norman period London acquired a new administrative and urbanistic structure. On Christmas Eve of 1066, William the Conqueror was crowned King of England and granted Londoners special privileges and greater autonomy in order to win their favor; however, he also built a new defensive fortress in order to control them. Following various later additions, the fortress is known today as the Tower of London: originally a royal residence, but over the course of the centuries a prison, a mint and even a zoo. The successor to William was responsible for the construction of Westminster Hall, next to the abbey, which formed the basis of Westminster Palace. This was the seat of government and attracted the elegant aristocratic palaces that sprung up around the Strand.

During the Middle Ages London became an independent municipality, and the Magna Carta granted by King John in 1215 ensured it the opportunity of electing a mayor each year. For two whole centuries the economy was in the hands of the merchants, united in guilds (the forerunners of the today's City Livery Companies). The great City markets of Smithfield, Billingsgate and Leadenhall offered goods from all over Europe, and the craftsmen were grouped into streets and districts, traces of which are still apparent in the street names today: Bread Street was the bakers' street and Threadneedle Street that of the tailors. The monastic orders also flourished during this period and the City boasted 13 monasteries. However, the Middle Ages were also a time of plagues and revolts. Between 1100 and 1300 the population grew to 50,000, but conditions of hygiene were disastrous. The City drew its water supply from the Thames and lacked a sewerage system; these factors aided the diffusion of bubonic plague, which had reached the country from European mainland. In just one year, between 1348 and 1349, the Black Death reduced the City's population by almost a third. The situation was compounded by the Peasants' Revolt in response to a poll tax introduced to subsidize the Hundred Years' War against France.

30 This Flemish miniature was made in Bruges around 1470. It depicts King Richard II being led to the Tower of London in 1399, after having been condemned as a tyrant.

31 top This print from a sixteenth-century engraving shows the Tower of London as it appeared in 1252. The building was constructed by William the Conqueror to dominate the City merchants.

31 bottom The history of London and the English people was recounted and illustrated by the historian and artist Matthew Paris

(d. 1259) in Historia Anglorum. *This page shows a man attempting to escape from the Tower of London by means of a rope made from knotted sheets.*

32 left This portrait, dating back to the first half of the nineteenth century, shows Henry VIII as Defender of the Faith. It was inspired by a mural at Hampton Court painted by Hans Holbein the Younger around the end of the fifteenth century.

32-33 This engraving shows the plan of London, surrounded by the City walls. The picture is from the first volume of Civitates Orbis Terrarum, published in Cologne in 1572: a six-volume atlas detailing the main cities of the world.

33 top This engraving by Czech artist Wenceslaus Hollar shows Whitehall Palace as it appeared in the seventeenth century, before it was destroyed by the fire of 1698. Today all that remains of the palace is Banqueting House.

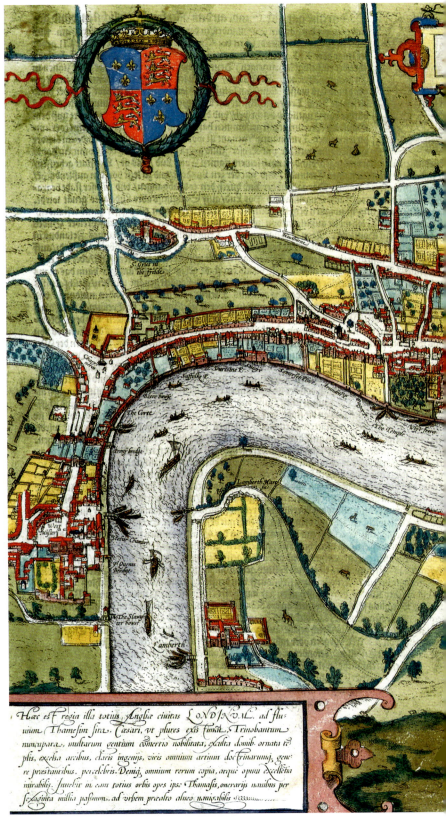

The Tudor dynasty was accompanied by important new changes, including the Reformation. In 1536, Henry VIII declared the break from the Church of Rome and proclaimed the birth of the Church of England. The move to Protestantism also changed the appearance of the City. The dissolution of the monasteries and confiscation of Church property made new land available, which the king granted to his supporters. The City started expanding again as the old religious buildings were demolished or converted into sanitariums, hospices or prisons, leaving traces of their presence only in place names, such as Blackfriars and Whitefriars. Henry VIII was a great patron and was responsible for much of the current appearance of Hampton Court, Lambeth Palace, Whitehall and the new residence of St. James's Palace, while what we now know as Hyde Park, Regent's Park, Greenwich and Richmond Parks are actually old royal hunting grounds.

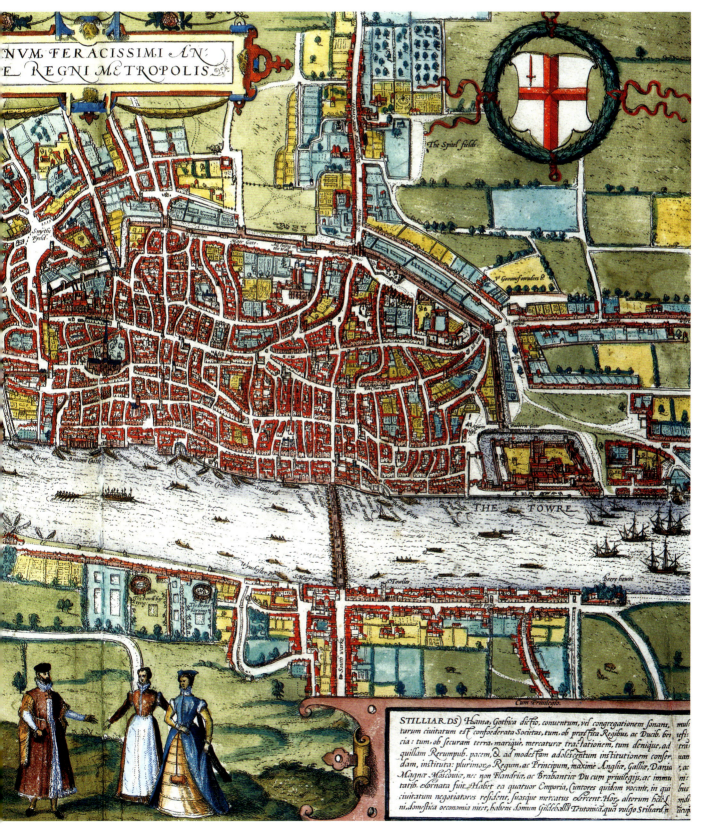

... NVM, FERACISSIMI AN-
E REGNI METROPOLIS &c.

The Spity fields.

Smythe Freld.

Black Freere Bayard Castle

Stilliardt

THE TOWRE

STILLIARDS) Hansa, Gothica dictio, conuentum, vel congregationem sonans,
tarum ciuitatum est confoederata Societas, tum, ob praefita Regibus, ac Ducib. ben-
cia: tum, ob securam terra, mariq́ue, mercaturæ tractationem, tum denique, ad
quillam Rerumpub. pacem, & ad modestam adolescentum institutionem confer-
dam, instituta: plurimor, Regum, ac Principum, maximè Angliæ, Galliæ, Daniæ
Magnæ Moscouiæ, nec non Flandriæ, ac Brabantiæ Du cum priuilegijs, ac immu-
tatib. Cornata fuit. Habet ea quatuor Emporia, Cuntores quidam vocant, in qua
ciuitatum negotiatores resident, suasque mercatus Cxercent. Hor. alterum hác
ni, domestica oeconomia nitet, habene domum Gildeballa Teutonica, quá vulgo Stiliard. n

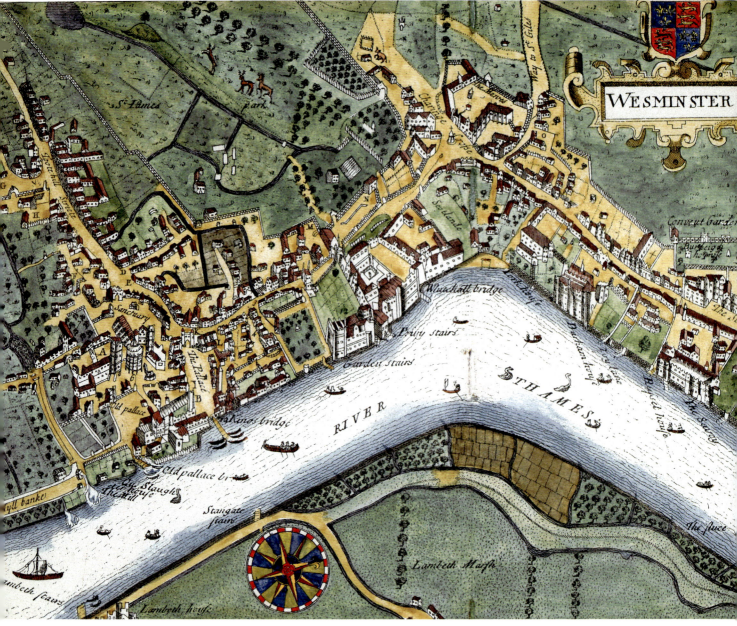

34 top This plate by the famous engraver Wenceslaus Hollar (1607-1677) shows Westminster Hall as it appeared in the seventeenth century. The Hall, built in 1097, is the only part of the original building to have survived the fires that destroyed the palace.

34-35 This copper engraving shows the plan of London around 1600. The City was expanding rapidly during this period and its population had reached approximately 75,000 in the City and 150,000 in the suburbs outside the walls.

35 top Very few pictures have survived of the original building of the Globe Theatre. This 1616 engraving shows the famous theatre following its reconstruction in 1614, after it had been destroyed by fire the previous year during a play.

35 bottom The Great Fire of 1666 was a disastrous event for London. This lithograph dating back to the second half of the seventeenth century effectively conveys the impression of a City devastated by the flames: over 80 churches and 13,000 houses were destroyed in five days.

The period of the Tudor dynasty also coincided with further mercantile expansion. The discovery of America and new trading routes in Africa and the Orient turned London into one of the most important European centers of trade, with a Royal Stock Exchange and important shipping companies that explored unknown lands in search of riches. The arts flourished along with the economy. The fashion for theater-going exploded during the reign of Elizabeth I, Henry's daughter. It became extremely popular with all social classes, despite being banned by the City authorities as it was considered a distraction from work. However, rather than closing down, the theaters eluded the bans by moving to the areas outside the City's jurisdiction on the south bank of the Thames. The Globe and The Rose are just two of the most famous playhouses built on the South Bank where the works of Shakespeare and Marlowe were staged around the end of the sixteenth century. In 1600, London was a City with over 200,000 inhabitants, divided among three main centers: the City, the heart of trade and finance; Westminster, the seat of political power with the es-

tate of St. James's established by Henry VIII; and Southwark, a burgeoning industrial pole that developed on the land confiscated from the Church.

The years of the Tudors marked a period of great change for the layout of the City. Urban planning was applied for the first time, using the Renaissance model to build wide, regular streets and new quarters laid out around squares, which became the focus of City life. London's spacious squares such as Leicester Square and Soho Square date back to this period. The architect responsible for this innovation was Inigo Jones. He produced the experimental design for Covent Garden, the Queen's House at Greenwich and the Banqueting House in Whitehall.

However, two catastrophes struck: the Great Plague of 1665 and just one year later the Great Fire, a disaster of devastating proportions that continued uninterrupted for three days. The damage was incredible: almost 100,000 victims were claimed by the plague and 80% of the walled City, which was mostly built of wood, was devoured by the flames, including 87 churches and 13,000 houses.

The GREAT FIRE of LONDON in the Year 1666.

The disaster left a permanent mark on the City's development. The Rebuilding Act of 1667 established that henceforth all buildings could only be made from brick and stone. The principal figure in the construction of the new London was Christopher Wren, who was responsible for 51 of the 54 churches that were rebuilt, including his masterpiece, the new St. Paul's, the first true Protestant cathedral.

Following the Great Fire many wealthy Londoners started to move out of the City, creating the residential quarters in the West End. The area to the south of the Thames also became more accessible owing to the construction of the Westminster and Blackfriars bridges. Up until that time London Bridge had been the only bridge over the river. In the mid-eighteenth century the City walls and the remaining gates were also demolished. Immigration, trade and expansion towards the colonies brought a new wave of wealth to the City, which was translated in opulent architecture financed by its rich families. Examples of such architecture are the current Somerset House and the monumental Bank of England. The new streets, squares and terraces of elegant townhouses built in the exclusive districts of Mayfair, Marylebone, Soho and Bloomsbury also date back to this period.

36 top The gardens of Hampton Court, shown here in an eighteenth-century picture, were designed in Renaissance style by Henry VIII and later converted to Baroque style between 1660 and 1702. George II subsequently added a mile-long canal, inspired by the gardens of Versailles.

36 bottom The Royal Hospital Chelsea was founded in 1682 by King Charles II as a home for war veterans and invalid soldiers. The building was designed by Christopher Wren and arranged around three sides of a quadrangle, with the southern side open onto the Thames, overlooking what were originally conceived as water gardens.

36-37 This picture shows the first building of the Royal Exchange, constructed in 1565 by Thomas Gresham and destroyed by the Great Fire of London in 1666. The second building, erected in 1838, was also destroyed by a fire and the current structure dates back to 1842.

37 top The imposing Tudor building known as Lambeth Palace has been the London residence of the Archbishop of Canterbury since 1197. It stands on the south bank of the Thames, opposite Westminster Abbey.

38-39 Eighteenth-century London, shown in this engraving, was a rapidly developing City. The walls had been demolished and the City was enjoying a period of flourishing trade, which resulted in a new building boom financed by wealthy families.

40 top The eighteenth century was a period of great expansion for London: the City grew along the northern bank of the Thames, as shown in this 1754 map that depicts the streets and buildings that appeared around the Tower of London.

40 bottom Somerset House was built around 1770 by the architect William Chambers to house government offices on a site between the river and the Strand. Despite subsequent alterations, the riverside façade, shown here in an early nineteenth-century print, remains the most majestic, just as Chambers had originally intended.

40-41 The Tower of London was built in the eleventh century by William the Conqueror and became the residence of Henry VII in 1485. It ceased to be used as a royal palace after his death and subsequently became a terrible prison, where Anne Boleyn was beheaded in 1536.

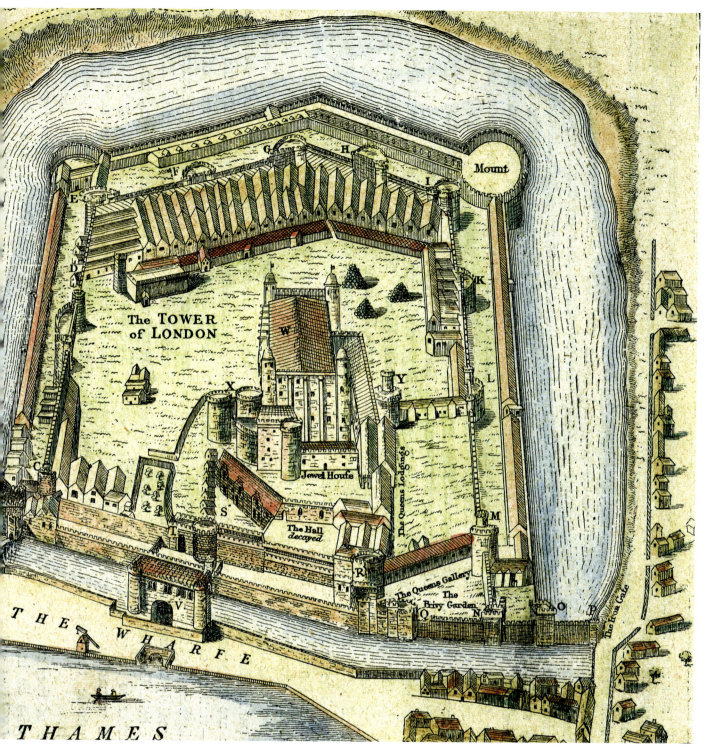

The TOWER
of LONDON

Mount

E
F
G
H
I
D
K
C
X
Y
L
W
S
M
T
R
The Hall
decayed
Jewel House
The Queens Lodgings
The Queens Gallery
The
Privy Garden
V
Q
N
O
P
The River Gate

THE WHARFE

THAMES

*41 bottom
Hundreds of years
had passed since
the construction of
the first bridge over
the Thames in the
twelfth century, and
by the nineteenth
century the river
had become
London's main
trading route, as
shown in this print
from the book
entitled Six Views
of the Metropolis,
published in 1804.*

42-43 This print of the Thames in the eighteenth century confirms the importance of the river as the focus of British trade during the period.

42 bottom left Soho Square, shown here in a 1754 color engraving, was built by Richard Frith on an area known as Kemps Field around 1677, while the central gardens were added in 1681. It was originally called King's Field, but was renamed during the eighteenth century.

42 bottom right The plan for St. James's Square, shown here in a 1700 engraving, dates back to 1670. It was one of the first squares in the City to be lined with elegant houses. Its current appearance is the result of changes made during the nineteenth century.

43 bottom Somerset House, shown here next to the Adelphi in a 1795 engraving, was built on the site of a Tudor palace that was demolished in 1775. The building was originally commissioned by William Robinson, but was subsequently built by William Chambers.

44 top Customs House, shown here in an 1828 print, was the building where the documents for the calculation of customs taxes on imports and exports were consigned. Taxes on trade constituted the City government's main source of income.

44 center Oxford Street, shown here in an 1815 engraving, was named after Oxford University. Despite its importance as a communications route, it did not assume the name and appearance of a proper street until 1877. Electric lighting was installed in 1899 and a tramline in January 1900.

The Victorian age represented a moment of strong contrasts for the City. The growing wealth of the City also led to a rapid increase in land prices, forcing the poorer citizens to move to the outskirts, where they were joined by heavy industry, which could no longer be contained within the City center. This was the London of the Industrial Revolution, but also of the social hardships described by Charles Dickens in his novels. The City was subdivided into areas that corresponded to distinct classes: the middle and upper classes inhabited the West End and Hampstead; whereas the working classes were confined to the East End, where they often lived in squalor. In 1800, London's population exceeded one million, making it the largest City in Europe. By 1837, five new bridges had been built over the Thames, but it was the railway more than any other factor that triggered the greatest urban expansion and the City's population reached six million by the end of the century.

These were the golden years of London's architecture. The man of the moment was John Nash, the architect who designed an ideal garden City with parks, lakes, townhouses and elegant palaces overlooking wide avenues and spacious squares. His most important projects include Regent Street, Trafalgar Square, Piccadilly Circus and Oxford Circus and the conversion of Buckingham House into a palace worthy of a king, i.e., Buckingham Palace. His style also influenced the construction of public buildings, such as the British Museum and the National Gallery, in neoclassical style.

44 bottom The Royal Opera House was designed by Edward Shepherd and built in 1728 in the elegant district of Covent Garden. It was initially known as the Covent Garden Theatre. The first building was destroyed in 1809 and rebuilt by Inigo Jones.

44-45 The British Museum was founded according to the posthumous wishes of the physician and naturalist Hans Sloane (1670-1753), who had compiled a collection of 71,000 pieces, a library and a herbarium during his lifetime. The museum was inaugurated in 1759 and was initially housed in the seventeenth-century building of Montagu House, on the site of the current museum (shown here in an 1862 print).

45 bottom
Buckingham House
was built in 1761
for the consort of
George III and
transformed into
Buckingham Palace
by the architect John
Nash in 1826, at a
staggering cost of
500,000 pounds.
Nash's design
eccentricities cost
him the job, and
William IV replaced
him with Edward
Blore in 1830.

46-47 This 1845
engraving shows a
panoramic view of
Victorian London.
This map is one of
over four million
maps and atlases
housed in the Map
Library, the
dedicated section of
the British Library
annexed to the
British Museum.

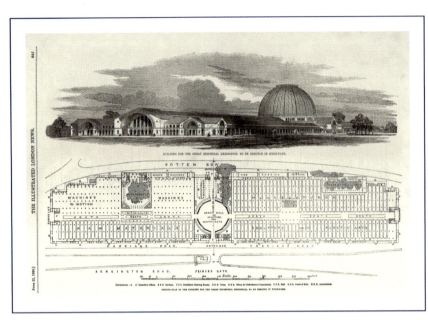

The Victorian age was also a glorious period for the country. Prince Albert, the consort of Queen Victoria, organized the Great Exhibition of 1851 in order to celebrate the grandeur of the new capital. The event was held in a magnificent iron and glass pavilion in Hyde Park. The favorite pastimes of the royal couple included the foundation of museums and concert halls, which were built on the new royal properties of South Kensington. Although built after his death, the Royal Albert Hall, the Victoria and Albert Museum and the Natural History Museum are three of the most significant cultural institutes proposed by Prince Albert, who is commemorated by a monument in Kensington Gardens.

48 top In 1852 the British crown decided to celebrate the indisputable political, economic and technological supremacy achieved by the Empire with the Great Exhibition. The map shows the plan of the pioneering iron and glass palace that was specially built to house the event in Hyde Park.

48 bottom Cannon Street Station, as it appeared at its inauguration in 1866. Today all that remains of the original structure are the two towers, due to German air raids during World War II.

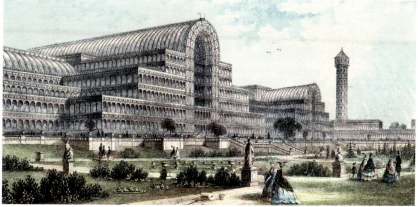

48-49 The fervent and chaotic activity of Smithfield Market—London's livestock market—was described by Charles Dickens in Oliver Twist. During Victorian times, around 1.5 million animals were sold there each year for a nineteenth-century value of eight million pounds.

49 bottom The Crystal Palace, designed by Joseph Paxton, was built in record time. The pavilion was formed by an iron frame clad with over 900,000 square feet of glass and was erected in just 10 days. The event was visited by over six million visitors.

50 top This
photograph of
Piccadilly Circus
taken in 1909
reveals how it was
already one of
London's busiest
junctions. The
famous nude

winged figure of
Eros, placed in
the square in
1893, symbolizes
the beginning
of the reaction to
the severe
austerity of the
Victorian Age.

50 center
Trafalgar Square
in a photograph
taken at the
beginning of the
twentieth century.
The square was
built in 1840 to a
design by the

royal architect John
Nash. Its central
position has always
made it a favorite
meeting place for
Londoners, who
traditionally
celebrate New Year's
Eve there.

50-51 Parliament Square and the 348-foot tower housing Big Ben, as they appeared in 1909, before the bomb damage of World War II.

51 The royal carriage of King George V and Queen Mary crossing Lambeth Bridge during the inauguration ceremony held on July 12, 1932.

The new demands of the increasing London traffic required the replacement of the previous bridge built in 1862, which was reserved for pedestrians only.

At the beginning of the twentieth century London's main thoughts turned to entertainment, in a natural reaction to the austerity of the Victorian age: the legendary Ritz Hotel opened in Piccadilly and the first American-style department stores such as Selfridges and Harrods appeared. Cars, the first motorbuses and trams also made their debut. However, this euphoria was short-lived. During the First World War London was bombed by Zeppelins. The Roaring Twenties, characterized by the quest for amusement, involved only a small privileged slice of society, while the rest of London's inhabitants fell victim to soaring inflation, aggravated by high unemployment. The situation came to a head in the General Strike of 1926, which paralyzed the City for nine days.

In an attempt to allay the crisis, London County Council tried to coordinate the development of the City with the introduction of welfare programs, commencing with the creation of public housing and new districts. The population had reached almost nine million by this stage, and the extension of the subway line enabled the expansion of the City into what was known as Metroland on its far northwestern outskirts where dormitory suburbs of terraced houses sprung up.

The crisis of the 1930s was only a foreshadowing of the disastrous events that the Second World War was to bring. The Blitz started in 1940. London was bombed continuously for 57 days and intermittently for another six months. By the end of the war one-third of the City and the entire East End and Docks had been destroyed. Of the 51 churches built by Christopher Wren, 17 were seriously damaged, although St. Paul's Cathedral was miraculously spared. Postwar immigration changed the appearance of the City. The "new English" came from the colonies of the British Empire and were attracted by the demand for labor at a time in which the City's population was drastically reduced, also as a result of migration towards the country. The Caribbean communities chose Notting Hill; the Indians, Southhall; immigrants from China and Hong Kong, Soho and Cypriots, Finsbury.

The whole country busied itself with reconstruction, the economy took off and London celebrated the recovery with the Festival of Britain in 1951. Exactly one hundred years had passed since the Great Exhibition and the South Bank Centre, a block of cement overlooking the Thames intended to represent a symbol of modernity, was built to host the festival.

52-53 This is how London appeared at the end of May 1945, after years of air strikes. St. Paul's Cathedral survived miraculously unscathed.

53 bottom left May 1945: Winston Churchill and other members of the Cabinet greet the rejoicing crowds from Whitehall following the defeat of Germany.

53 bottom right This photograph shows Piccadilly Circus crowded with people celebrating VE Day on 16 May, 1945. The war was over and the illuminated signs could once again shine above the square. The statue of Eros, which had been protected against the air raids by a heavy wooden frame, resumed its watch over the square.

54 *This is how Heathrow Airport appeared to approaching aircraft ion 1968. The runways resemble a geometric pattern in this photograph taken from a height of around 13,000 feet.*

54-55 A crowd of approximately a million people, according to police estimates, thronged the Mall in front of Buckingham Palace on occasion of the Party at the Palace organized to celebrate the Queen's Golden Jubilee on June 4, 2002.

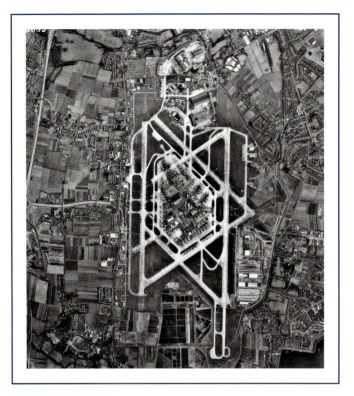

The coronation ceremony of Queen Elizabeth II in 1953 was an historic date for the whole world and marked the first Eurovision broadcast. Swinging London arrived with the advent of the 1960s and became the world capital of music and fashion. The Beatles' records and Mary Quant's miniskirts were the latest rages, legendary Carnaby Street became the meeting place for young hippies and boutiques offering the very latest fashions opened in King's Road.

The age of the Beatles ended with the Fab Four's last album and the quest for fun that had characterized the past two decades disappeared in the 1970s. This period of economic crisis and social protest was marked by inflation, the oil crisis and the first IRA bombings, while the trendy shop windows of the King's Road were replaced by the first punks.

The Eighties went down in history as the decade of Thatcherism. Margaret Thatcher, Great Britain's first woman Prime Minister, was elected in 1979 and immediately became famous for her conservative politics. In order to curb the serious recession, Margaret Thatcher made cuts to all the social services, increasing the class divide. This was a golden period for the yuppies: the old Victorian and Georgian houses in the City center were restored and converted into luxurious homes, and what had been considered outlying districts, such as Clapham and Paddington, also became residential. This process of gentrification enabled the middle class to settle the working-class quarters of the City center; however, for others unemployment and housing shortages gave rise to the cardboard cities around Waterloo Bridge and even on the Strand, where the homeless took shelter beneath newspapers and sleeping bags. One of the most unpopular decisions of the Iron Lady was the abolition in 1986 of the Greater London Council, headed by the highly popular Ken Livingstone, promoter of populist measures including the introduction of re-

duced fares for public transport. For years London remained the only European capital without its own administrative body and mayor. However, the wheel turns and fourteen years later, in 2000, Livingstone reappeared in the role of mayor at the head of the Greater London Assembly, the City's current administrative body. In 2004 Livingstone was re-elected for a second term.

The latest important changes are recent history. London was given a facelift in preparation for the Millennium and the new projects of urban rebirth were partially funded with income from the National Lottery. Work commenced with the Docklands, one of the projects formerly promoted by Margaret Thatcher, for the creation of a new office district on the Isle of Dogs but was abandoned several times.

Southwark and South Bank, the area south of the Thames that had always been neglected due to its reputation as a rough neighborhood, underwent a redevelopment program that made it into the City's most exciting district, with buildings by internationally renowned architects A futuristic new pedestrian bridge across the Thames connects this new London to the City, the old factories have been transformed into exclusive lofts or reconverted into museums—as in the case of the Tate Modern—and new construction sites are awaiting the opportunity to work definitive change on the area. Other cultural institutions throughout the City have been invested with the same spirit of renewal and have been modernized with new additions, such as the Great Court of the British Museum, or simply renovated. The massive and controversial Millennium Dome on the far eastern stretch of the Thames in Greenwich is the symbol of London's rebirth. This "cathedral" of the future was inaugurated in 2000 and, following the great celebrations to mark the passage of the new millennium, is currently waiting to discover its next destination.

55 bottom left The King George V Dock—the third of the Royal Docks—was built in 1921 to extend the trade concentrated around the Royal Victoria and Albert Docks. It was designed with the requirements of modern shipping in mind and equipped with the latest technologies and facilities.

55 bottom right The Festival of Britain was organized in 1951 to celebrate the centenary of the Great Exhibition. The opening ceremony was presided by George VI, who also inaugurated the Royal Festival Hall on the South Bank for the occasion.

BETWEEN THE CITY

AND WESTMINSTER

One square mile: that's the size of the City of London, the center of trade and finance but above all the capital's original nucleus. London was born here, yet what we see today is the result of three fairly recent stages of City planning, following the devastation of the Great Fire of 1666 that destroyed four-fifths of the area: the expansion of the Victorian period in the second half of the nineteenth century, the post-war reconstruction and, finally, the building boom of the 1980s, when half the office blocks visible today were erected. The result is an unusually modern impact upon what should be the capital's "historic center". However, the contemporary landmarks, such as Richard Rogers' Lloyds Building or Norman Foster's Swiss Re Tower, counterbalance the ancient remains of a more remote past, commencing with St. Paul's Cathedral, Christopher Wren's most imposing work. This unmistakable feature of the London skyline was built in 1675 and boasts a majestic dome, second in size only to that of St Peter's in Rome. Little trace, however, remains of the City's Roman origins, with the exception of London Bridge, the first passage across the Thames built by the Romans. The original wooden structure disappeared long ago and was replaced with a more solid reinforced concrete bridge in practically the same position. The Temple of Mithras is wedged between the office blocks on Queen Victoria Street, and the statues that once adorned it can be seen in the Museum of London. The City has a strange atmosphere because, although teeming with 500,000 people during the day, it turns into a ghost town at night, with a population of just 5,000 residents. Old customs and institutions survive in this district, such as the Guildhall, which was the seat of municipal government for eight centuries and is still the headquarters of the Corporation of London. This body is headed by the Lord Mayor, whose jurisdiction is limited to the City alone and who still enjoys the special status granted by William the Conqueror. The Royal Stock Exchange and the Bank of England, two symbols of the British economy, face the City's most beautiful square, the appropriately named Bank. The eastern boundary of the City of London is marked by the monumental Tower of London, which overlooks Tower Bridge, the City's most photographed bridge with its Neo-Gothic towers. Upon completion in 1078, the tower was the City's highest building, at 130 feet.

The City of Westminster officially commences beyond the Temple Bar Memorial, but despite its actual boundaries, everyone considers Westminster to be the area immediately surrounding the Abbey and the Houses of Parliament—the center of royal, political and religious power for the past thousand years. Edward the Confessor transferred the royal residence here from the City in the eleventh century and founded the largest abbey in England, right next to his palace. The huge Neo-Gothic Palace of Westminster, designed by the Victorian architect Charles Barry and better known as the Houses of Parliament, rises from the bank of the Thames with its famous clock tower, Big Ben. Nearby Westminster Abbey looks almost small in comparison. This majestic Gothic building is the burial place of the English royal family and the site of almost all coronations since the times of William the Conqueror. Whitehall, wedged between two buildings, is more than simply the street connecting Parliament Square to Trafalgar Square. It was already the site of most of the country's government buildings by the nineteenth century, giving rise to a geographical division of the institutions that still survives today: Westminster for politicians and Whitehall for civil servants. This imposing avenue embellished with statues and monuments is lined with the power centers of the past and present, such as Banqueting House, England's earliest Palladian building, built by Inigo Jones, and the sole surviving portion of the larger Whitehall Palace, the permanent residence of the English monarchs until it was partially destroyed in a fire. And, of course, there is

---

56-57 from left to right Tower Bridge; the impressive Swiss Re Tower; the loop in the Thames with

Tower Bridge in the background on the left; the unmistakable architecture of Westminster Palace and Westminster Bridge.

59 The clock housed in the tower of the Palace of Westminster is the largest in Britain, with four faces

measuring 23 feet across and a 14-foot minute hand. It has been keeping time for the entire nation since 1859.

Downing Street, where the seventeenth-century townhouse at number ten has been the residence for each British Prime Minister since 1732.

The beginning of the West End is marked by Trafalgar Square, the unmistakable landmark with the column supporting the statue of Admiral Nelson. Though still within the boundaries of Westminster, this area has a different atmosphere. Not only is it the land of shopping and entertainment, but it is also home to important museums, famous monuments and some of London's most elegant districts. The great neoclassical complex that occupies much of the square was built in 1834 to house the National Gallery, an appropriate showcase for one of the world's most important art collections. Behind it is Leicester Square, which has been the focus of the City's entertainment since the nineteenth century. It is still lit up today with the signs of cinemas and discos and borders on the districts of Soho and Covent Garden.

Soho developed on the land confiscated from the Church by Henry VIII and was one of the first residential areas for the eighteenth-century nobility before it became a mecca for those seeking entertainment and transgression. As the wealthy classes gradually moved further west, the elegant homes gave way to bars frequented by intellectuals of all kinds, and a red-light district grew up and still survives today in the little lanes around the main thoroughfare, Old Compton Street. Frith Street, Dean Street and Wardour Street boast incredible numbers of bars, restaurants and dubious locales, but also film offices, interrupted only by Berwick Street Market, a seemingly unlikely fruit and vegetable market right in the City center. The enclave of Chinatown, nestling between Leicester Square and Shaftesbury Avenue, is a world unto itself. The imitation Oriental gates, pagoda-shaped telephone boxes and red lanterns illuminating the numerous restaurants lining Gerrard Street have made these three small blocks a picturesque tourist attraction that is also very popular with Londoners.

Covent Garden has been one of the centers of the capital ever since it was founded. During the first half of the seventeenth century the architect Inigo Jones transformed the old vegetable garden of a medieval convent into what was to become London's first real square, enclosed between elegant terraces (Victorian townhouses) and St. Paul's Cathedral. Over the years the square became a meeting place for intellectuals seeking recreation in the inns of the area or at one of the many theaters that grew up around the neoclassical Royal Opera House. The Victorian age saw the inauguration here of London's largest and most famous fruit and vegetable market, which occupied the square before being transferred elsewhere between the 1970's and 1980's. The area was subsequently converted into a lively shopping and entertainment center, with restaurants, boutiques and bookshops, concentrated around the pedestrian zone of Neal Street and Neal's Yard.

The Strand marks the southern boundary of the West End. This street was once located on the bank of the Thames and assumed its current appearance during Victorian times. During the late twelfth century the local nobility built their luxury residences here, with gardens facing the river's "beach", making the street connecting Westminster to the City one of London's most sought-after residential areas, which was soon also colonized by teahouses, restaurants and exclusive hotels. Today the Strand is a street just over half a mile long, which preserves only a few traces of its past glory: the Palladian Somerset House, with one side facing onto the current riverbank, the Gothic building of the Royal Courts of Justice and London's most luxurious hotel, the Savoy, built in 1889 on the ashes of the medieval Savoy Palace.

60 The dome of St. Paul's Cathedral is 360 feet tall and second in size only to that of St. Peter's in Rome. It rests on a colonnade, which is surmounted in turn by a stone gallery that offers spectacular views over the City and the Thames.

62 The Thames is the longest river in England, with a total length of 215 miles. Around 30 miles of the London stretch are plied by passenger boats.

63 top Tower Bridge has a total length of 2,640 feet. Its two central spans can be opened in one and a half minutes to allow the passage of ships. This operation is now performed about 500 times a year, although it was carried out 50 times a day during its period of greatest use. An elevated walkway enables the passage of pedestrians even when the bridge is raised. Today the bridge's history is documented in the Tower Bridge Experience exhibition housed in the two towers.

63 bottom Tower Bridge is the last of the 33 bridges that cross the London stretch of the Thames. However, its current red, white and blue colors do not correspond to the original version of the building, which was gray. A boat trip along the Thames enables tourists to admire the historic buildings and, more recently, the spectacular new contemporary architecture that lines the riverbanks.

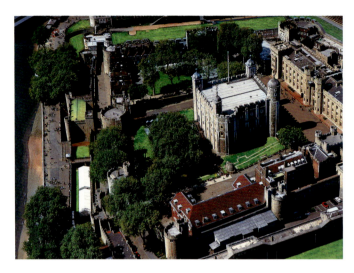

64 The White Tower is the oldest remaining building of the Tower of London, commenced by William the Conqueror in 1077. It has always been used as an armory and is still home to a large part of the national collection of weapons and armor. The Tower of London is not only famous as a former prison and place of execution of traitors, but also as the home of the Crown Jewels.

65 The Tower of London was built in the years following 1066 by William the Conqueror and is a veritable medieval fortress in the midst of the City. It houses a palace, prisons, chapels and museums. Eighteen families still live here, making the Tower the smallest village in the City.

66 top This little square with a commemorative column is situated on the northern side of St. Paul's Cathedral.

66-67 St. Paul's Cathedral was built by the architect Christopher Wren and modeled on an Italian palace, with a

Latin cross plan. Its semicircular southern portico (foreground) is said to have been copied from a Baroque church in Rome.

67 St. Paul's Cathedral is the mother church of the Diocese of London and the church of Londoners. It is the only English

cathedral with a dome, which can be seen from far off, even from the opposite side of the river, in the area south of the Thames.

68 The Bank of
England is the
heart of the British
economy and the
City. It is so
important that it
has given its name
to the crossroads
at which it stands
and the subway
station, both of
which are known
simply as Bank.
The main streets
of the City meet
here.

69 The Strand once
connected the Thames
to the road that led
out of the City and
was lined with
restaurants, hotels
and theaters in
Victorian times.
Today it runs parallel
to the river and
connects Trafalgar
Square and Fleet
Street. Some of the
luxury houses built
during that period can
still be seen.

70 Next to the massive Bank of England stands another institution of financial London: the Royal Exchange, which was founded in Tudor times and has been the focus of the City's trade ever since. The current building with Corinthian portico dates back to 1844 and is the third to occupy the original site.

71 Today only the outer wall remains of the original Bank of England building designed in 1788 by John Sloane, for the rest was demolished during the 1920s

when the bank was extended. The new building houses a museum that documents the history of the institution.

72-73 The small crescent-shaped "island" behind the Strand is occupied by buildings that were constructed at the beginning of the twentieth century and enclosed by a crescent-shaped street called Aldwych, after an ancient Danish colony. The complex is bounded by the buildings of India House and Australia House.

74 The skyline of the modern City is characterized by high skyscrapers that rise above the low buildings of the historic district. The latest addition is the curious gherkin-shaped tower designed by Norman Foster, which is over 590 feet high.

75 This reinforced concrete skyscraper, built in 1986 by the British architect Richard Rogers, houses the headquarters of the famous Lloyds insurance company. One of the peculiarities of the building is that its water pipes, heating system, stairs and elevators are all located on the outside. The tower is surmounted by a 197-foot glass barrel vault, which is visible in the photograph.

76-77 Finsbury Circus, in the center of the City, is the only square in London to have preserved its green. Office workers gather here to play bowls or relax in the shade of the trees during their lunchbreak.

78 The Swiss Re Tower, at number 30 St. Mary Axe, has 40 floors served by 16 elevators. Its shape and large glass windows enable the interiors to benefit from all-round natural light.

79 The most curious of the new buildings that have changed the City skyline is the skyscraper built by Norman Foster for the Swiss Re insurance company, which Londoners have wittily nicknamed "The Gherkin".

80-81 The dome of St. Paul's Cathedral no longer dominates the London skyline. This honor has fallen to the City's modern skyscrapers, such as the rounded Swiss Re Tower— the latest arrival—and Tower 42, the tallest in the City at 600 feet.

82 The crossings over the Thames by the Tate Modern are known as Blackfriars Bridges. The two Victorian metal road and railway bridges have recently been joined by a pedestrian bridge (not visible in the picture) that leads directly to the square in front of the gallery.

83 The modern Cannon Street Station was inaugurated in 1866, but rebuilt during the 1960s. Today the two red-brick side towers are all that remain of the original building.

84-85 This spectacular panoramic view shows the City, on the left of the Thames, with Tower Bridge in the background.

86-87 This photograph shows the Thames winding its way westwards. The Millennium Wheel is visible in the background.

88 Covent Garden is the name of this square designed by Inigo Jones at the beginning of the seventeenth century, which was modeled on the great squares of Rome and Paris. Today it is a complex dedicated to shopping and entertainment in the heart of the City.

89 The National Gallery, at the bottom of the photograph, was built in 1838 at the same time as Trafalgar Square, and was gradually extended as its collection grew. Rooms were added to the eastern wing around 1872, while the central pavilion was enlarged a decade later and the western and northern wings extended at the beginning of the twentieth century.

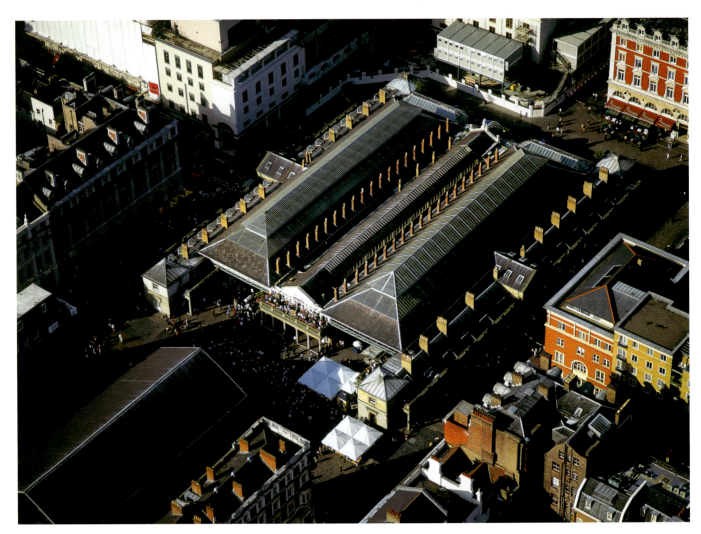

90 The Central
Market Building,
which used to house
the market, is
composed of three
parallel structures
supported by
colonnades and
joined by a glass
roof. The building
dates back to 1830.

91 Covent Garden
square is largely
occupied by what
used to be the old
covered market,
which now houses
cafés, restaurants
and unusual shops.

92 Trafalgar Square was built in 1820. It was designed by John Nash as an open space behind Charing Cross, although the buildings that line it are the subsequent work of other architects.

93 Nelson's Column dominates the center of Trafalgar Square. It is 144 feet high and topped with a statue of the famous admiral. The monument was completed in 1843 and the four bronze lions at its base added in 1867. The fountains are more recent, dating back to 1939.

94-95 The current Church of St. Martin-in-the-Fields (right in the photograph) was designed by James Gibbs and built in 1721. It stands in the corner of Trafalgar Square, on a site that has housed a church since the thirteenth century.

96 The riverside
façade of
Westminster Palace
is almost 1,000 feet
long. It constitutes
a spectacular sight
from the riverbank,
although the best
view can be enjoyed
from nearby
Westminster
Bridge.

97 The current
Westminster Palace
is not the original
building constructed
by William the
Conqueror. Indeed,
the first palace was
destroyed by a fire
in 1834 and a new
one was built in its
place, maintaining
the same plan.

98 Westminster Abbey is the largest of London's great churches. It was founded around 730 AD, but its current appearance dates back to the thirteenth century, when it was rebuilt in Gothic style by Henry de Reynes. Almost all the English monarchs were crowned in this church.

99 Majestic Westminster Palace was designed by Charles Barry and Augustus Welby and has 1,200 rooms, 11 courtyards, 100 flights of stairs and almost two miles of corridors.

100-101 Lambeth Palace, situated in the district of Lambeth on the south bank of the Thames, is the sole surviving example of the exclusive palaces that once lined the river. The complex is composed of several buildings from different periods, the oldest of which date back to the Middle Ages.

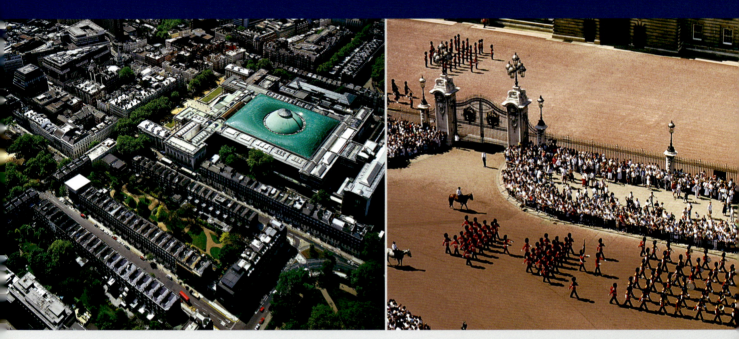

PICCADILLY AND

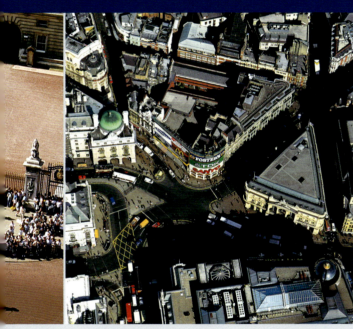

THE WEST END

Piccadilly, the main street of the West End, leads to the elegant districts of St. James's and Mayfair, which developed in the late seventeenth century as the City's first real residential suburbs. Henry VIII built the royal residence of St. James's Palace here and at the end of the eighteenth century the City's aristocracy followed his example. St. James's Square and St. James's Street were among the first roads to be built. Buckingham House, situated on the banks of the Tyburn River and later transformed into Buckingham Palace, and Burlington House, now the home of the Royal Academy, were among the most magnificent buildings constructed between Piccadilly and Hyde Park Corner. The following two centuries transformed the surrounding streets into the most luxurious in the capital, teeming with elegant stores, luxury hotels and gentlemen's clubs. Piccadilly became the smartest shopping street and the Mall, stretching from Buckingham Palace to Admiralty Arch, one of the grandest avenues. The area became studded with aristocratic homes overlooking Hyde Park. Regent's Street was designed by John Nash, the architect of the Prince Regent (the future George IV), as a triumphant street that was to lead to Regent's Park, and subsequently became one of the most fashionable streets, with stores, restaurants and theaters. Finally, the Adam brothers designed Portland Place, which was once London's widest street, and lined it with buildings in the brothers' distinctive style, featuring fanlights and wrought-iron railings. Although Piccadilly is no longer the street it once was and the aristocracy has departed,

Mayfair and St. James's have kept their reputations as London's most exclusive suburbs. The districts are criss-crossed by a grid network of streets that converge into large squares, which are home to hotels and embassies, and that have become legendary addresses: Savile Row, the street of custom tailors, Bond Street and Cork Street with their great auction houses and art galleries and some of the most classic symbols of the City: the statue of Eros in Piccadilly Circus, the enchanting St. James's Park and Green Park and, of course, Buckingham Palace.

The old Roman road to Oxford has always been one of London's most famous streets. Oxford Street has been dedicated to purchases since the early nineteenth century and today is a two-mile stretch of stores featuring many legendary names in shopping, such as Selfridges. It marks the boundary between the West End and Marylebone, the last district to be occupied by the aristocracy after Mayfair and St. James's. The area once housed one of the hunting reserves of Henry VIII: Marylebone Park, now known as Regent's Park, was designed by John Nash to house the residence of the Prince Regent and over 50 townhouses. The original plans were considerably rescaled but the park has preserved a grand appearance. During the Georgian and, subsequently, Victorian periods, new buildings were constructed north of popular Oxford Street and around Cavendish Square. Over the years the area has been transformed into an expanse of offices, boutiques and exclusive restaurants, interspersed with a few tourist attractions that nonetheless draw great crowds, from Madame Tussaud's wax-

102-103 from left to right
The unmistakable dome of the British Museum; the Changing of the Guard in front of Bucking Palace;

an overhead view of Piccadilly Circus; Buckingham Palace with the marble Queen Victoria Memorial on the right.

105 When it was first built at the beginning of the eighteenth century, Buckingham Palace was actually called Buckingham House and was a simple brick residence.

It was transformed into a palace worthy of a king in 1825 by John Nash, who clad the façade with stone and added the imposing entrance portico.

works to the Wallace Collection, housed in a small seventeenth-century French castle.

During the second half of the seventeenth century the Duke of Southampton started to build up the rural area north of Oxford Street, erecting new models of buildings laid out around geometrical squares, which are the distinctive feature of the area. The first was what is now Bloomsbury, followed in 1800 by Bedford Square, Brunswick Square and Russell Square. Bloomsbury and neighboring Fitzrovia have always been closely associated with art and culture: the quarter was the birthplace of the Bloomsbury Group, the group of unconventional artists who proclaimed the superiority of aesthetics over ethics at the beginning of the twentieth century. It has been home to intellectuals of the caliber of Charles Dickens, George Bernard Shaw, Karl Marx and, more recently, Dylan Thomas and George Orwell, keen patrons of the Fitzroy Tavern, which gave the district its name. The area has also spawned prestigious publishing houses and important cultural institutions, including the University of London. However, Bloomsbury is first and foremost associated with the British Museum, one of the most important museums in

the world, housed in a Grecian-style building with an Ionic portico and a huge colonnade that was built in 1823. The latest addition is the futuristic glass and steel roof above the Great Hall, designed by the British architect Norman Foster. Behind the museum, which houses extensive collections of ancient art and the precious Round Reading Room—the former home of the British Library—is an enormous university complex, which has practically engulfed several of the district's most attractive squares, lined with elegant Georgian houses. Beyond the boundaries of the university, busy Euston Road is home to another famous institution: the new British Library, a red-brick building that has received much criticism for its obsolete style, but which nonetheless conceals pleasant ultra-modern interiors.

Today Fitzrovia, concentrated around Tottenham Court Road and Charlotte Street, is a relatively quiet area formed by a dense network of streets and alleys lined with stores and restaurants. Its bohemian atmosphere has been partially modified by the modern reconstruction of the postwar period, whose most visible signs are Brunswick Square and the British Telecom Tower.

106 Piccadilly Circus is highly evocative, especially in the evening, when the square's distinctive neon signs are lit. London's first illuminated advertising sign made its debut here in 1932.

107 The triple archway of Admiralty Arch marks the entrance to The Mall, the avenue leading to Buckingham Palace designed by Aston Webb in 1910.

108-109 St. James's Park is London's oldest park and is situated between Buckingham Palace and the Treasury (foreground). It is home to a lake bordered by willow, fig and plane trees.

110 The long avenue known as The Mall commences at the Queen Victoria Memorial opposite Buckingham Palace. It was laid out for the Stuarts in the seventeenth century and subsequently converted into a processional route. It runs along the entire length of St. James's Park as far as the Horseguards Building, before proceeding to Trafalgar Square.

111 The Queen's Apartments, composed of a dozen rooms, are located on the northern side of Buckingham Palace, overlooking Green Park. The State Rooms have been open to the public since 1992 and comprise the Blue, White and Green Drawing Rooms, Music Room and Ballroom.

112-113 The Changing of the Guard ceremony is held when the queen is in residence, as indicated by the royal flag that flies above the palace façade. The parade either takes place every day or every other day.

114 The Reading Room, annexed to the British Museum, is open to the public and is covered by a large glass roof. The circular room was built in 1837 and can accommodate up to 400 readers. Over a million books are housed on its 21 miles of shelves.

115 London has few tall buildings, apart from those in the City and the new Docklands area. This photograph shows the Centrepoint.

116-117 The British Museum was restyled and modernized on occasion of the new millennium. The focus of the new design, the central Great Court, was completely cleared except for the circular Reading Room and covered with a spectacular glass roof by the architect Norman Foster.

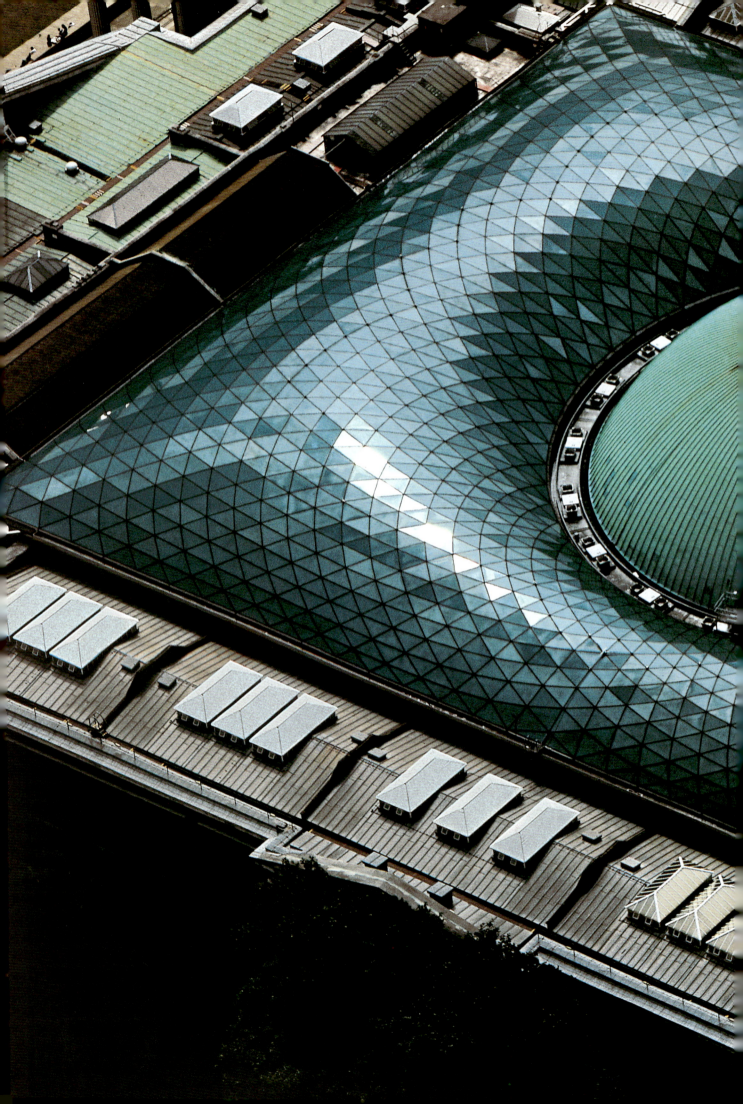

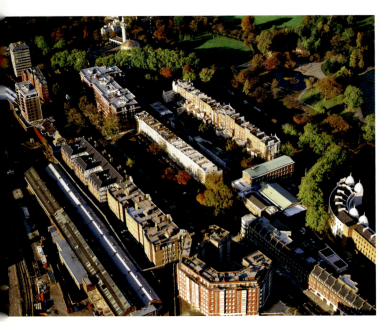

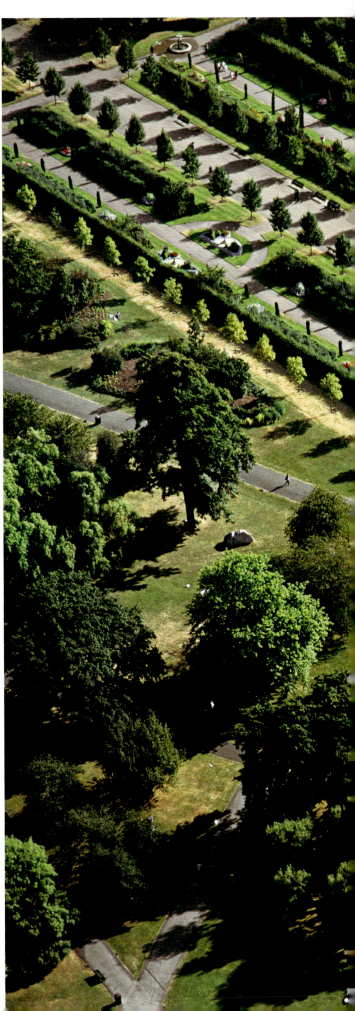

118 Regent's Park was built by John Nash around an irregularly shaped lake. Elegant terraced houses were built around the edge of the park, enclosed by a circular road, with the aim of transforming the park into a garden City.

118-119 The most surprising aspect of Regent's Park is the variety to be found within its 500-acre area, from the ancient horse-chestnut trees lining Broad Walk to Queen Mary's Rose Garden and the rock gardens, for the park contains a total of 30,000 plants.

120-121 This evocative nighttime view shows the lights of the City center.

122 Regent Street was designed by John Nash at the beginning of the nineteenth century and is the epitome of West End elegance. Today this street with wide sidewalks is one of London's main shopping streets.

123 Eros is the symbol of Piccadilly Circus. However, despite the popular name of the nude statue, it actually depicts the Christian angel of Charity. The aluminum figure was created by Alfred Gilbert and erected in the square in 1893, during the Victorian period, causing a great outcry from the conservatives.

124-125 Grosvenor Square is still one of the favorite spots of the City's American residents. This preference dates back to 1785, when it was inhabited by the first American ambassador in London and future US President, John Adams. The area is also known as "Little America" for the same reason.

125 Only eight of the 56 villas and crescents designed by John Nash for Regent's Park were ever built. The northern edge of the park has barely been touched, while most of the beautiful Regency-style terraces are concentrated towards the south and sides of the park.

126 The district of Belgravia developed at the beginning of the nineteenth century around the elegant residences that already occupied Chelsea and Kensington. It was the last project devised by the rich for the rich, with beautiful Regency-style buildings that were erected around Belgravia Square.

127 Oxford Circus is situated at the intersection of Regent Street and Oxford Street. The latter is considered London's main shopping street and is home to some of the City's most famous department stores, such as Selfridges, founded in 1908, and Marks and Spencer.

WESTERN

GRANDEUR

The districts of Victoria, Pimlico and Belgravia, wedged between the Thames and the gardens surrounding Buckingham Palace, perhaps boast the greatest number of luxury houses in London, inhabited by wealthy locals and foreigners, and are home to embassies and some of the City's most exclusive hotels. They developed when the aristocracy had already started to abandon the residential quarter of Mayfair. The evolution of the neighborhood represents a particularly important chapter in London's City-planning history. Indeed, Belgravia is the fruit of an ambitious project devised by the wealthy (the Grosvenor family) for the wealthy that was commenced in 1824 when the owners of this huge property commissioned the architect Thomas Cubitt to develop the area. The results were the beautiful white buildings decorated with stuccowork and arranged around the perfect flowerbeds that are still the distinctive feature of this district. They can be admired during a stroll along Belgrave Road, Belgrave Square and Eaton Square, amidst the highest expressions of elegance of the neighborhood. Following the success of the project, Cubitt commenced work on the nearby area of Pimlico, where refined Italianate palaces with elegant stuccowork are aligned around Warwick Square and Ecclestone Square. Development continued with the creation of Victoria Station, the point of arrival or departure for many travelers. Towards the end of the century, the old Millbank Prison was converted to house the National Gallery of British Art (now the Tate Britain).

The Royal Borough is the district of Kensington and Chelsea, a vast area that comprises other well-known quarters, including Knightsbridge and Notting Hill. It was founded at the end of the seventeenth century when William of Orange invited Christopher Wren and Nicholas Hawksmoor to transform his residence into the more majestic Kensington Palace, situated in Hyde Park, or more precisely in that half of the park that subsequently became known as Kensington Gardens. The king's presence attracted the aristocracy, who started to build residential palaces and the new Holland Park. During the nineteenth century the area was home to London's finest streets: Kensington Palace Gardens, Kensington High Street and Kensington Church Street are just a few examples. However, the boom only arrived with the Great Exhibition of 1851. The proceeds from the event were used to purchase the land where three great museums were built: the Victoria & Albert Museum, the Natural History Museum and the Science Museum. They occupy a huge complex composed of impressively large buildings, which is completed by the Royal Albert Hall, a Renaissance-style concert hall featuring an iron and glass dome and faced in red brick, the distinctive architectural feature of the district. Neighboring Knightsbridge also felt the influence of the Great Exhibition and was transformed from open country into a fashionable district. Ever since this time, the entire area has been an important shopping center, with the most famous addresses in Brompton Road.

In the southern part of the district, Chelsea had been the countryside of London's nobility since the time of Henry VIII. During the nineteenth century it attracted artists and intellectuals and became the focal point for new trends in the twentieth century. Although the King's Road is no longer the unconventional and cutting-edge street that it was at the time of Swinging London, the district has preserved its exclusive, fashionable air, with its riverside houses and many art galleries. Following its launch by the film of the same name, Notting Hill is now an expanse of terraced houses with pretty gardens and, above all, a myriad of trendy locales that have sprung up around Portobello Road, the site of one of the most famous markets in the world.

128-129 from left to right The green areas of Hyde Park and Kensington Gardens; the imposing buildings of the Natural History Museum; the Royal Albert Hall; Kensington Palace, designed by Christopher Wren, in Kensington Gardens.

130 Despite having been constructed during the Victorian period, the circular building of the Royal Albert Hall was inspired by the Renaissance style. Its red-brick façade with terracotta friezes is surmounted by a metal dome.

132 Hyde Park is one of Londoners' favorite spots for leisure or sport. The Serpentine Lido was built on the edge of the lake for those wishing to swim, row and even get a suntan in the summer.

133 At the beginning of the seventeenth century the district of Kensington lay outside London and was a favorite royal country retreat. It is now situated in the City center, on the edge of Hyde Park and Kensington Gardens.

134-135 Hyde Park was divided into two sections during the eighteenth century and the westernmost part has since been known as Kensington Gardens.

The two areas are divided by the Ring, the road that connects their respective entrances, known as Alexandra Gate and Victoria Gate.

135 Despite being a residential district, Kensington is also famous for its streets lined with elegant hotels and stores. Kensington High Street is one of the London's busiest shopping streets.

136-137 Together with Chelsea, Kensington forms the Royal Borough, which dates back to the Victorian period. It is one of London's most elegant areas, characterized by refined Victorian architecture and handsome stores.

138 top This late nineteenth-century building was built in Romanesque style and houses the Natural History Museum.

138 bottom The Victoria and Albert Museum is considered the world's greatest decorative-arts museum, with a collection that ranges from design to photography.

139 The Royal Albert Hall was designed to host cultural events. It was built by Queen Victoria's consort, Prince Albert, and is situated in the area nicknamed Albertopolis, due to the cultural institutions that the Prince founded there.

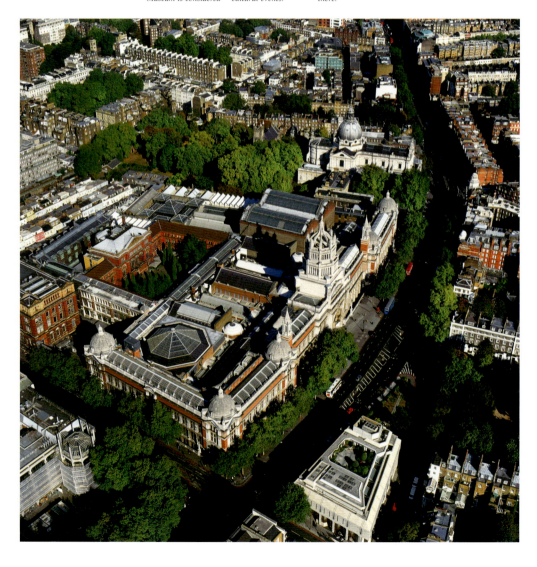

140 A triumphal arch stands at Hyde Park Corner, the main entrance situated on the southeastern side of the park. It was built in 1825 to mark the royal road between Kensington Palace and Hyde Park and transferred to its current position in 1883.

141 Hyde Park is just one of the City's 1,700 parks, which cover a total area of approximately 65 square miles. London already boasted large green parks in medieval times, but they were chiefly hunting reserves.

142 and 143
Kensington
Palace, in
Kensington
Gardens, became
a royal country
residence in 1689.
Its red-brick eastern
and southern
façades were
designed by
Christopher Wren.

144 top The Roman Catholic Westminster Cathedral was built in 1895 in Neo-Byzantine style, with a dome-topped campanile, and contrasts with the surrounding modern buildings.

144-145 Modern Victoria Station is actually the result of the union of two stations: the London Brighton South Coast Railway and the London, Chatham and Dover Railway, which were joined in 1924. Around 110 million passengers pass through the station each year.

145 South Kensington is the district situated between Hyde Park and Chelsea. It was largely built during the second half of the nineteenth century and is characterized by the Victorian style of its buildings. It is home to some of the City's foremost cultural institutes, such as the Royal Albert Hall, Victoria and Albert Museum and Natural History Museum.

TO THE

NORTH AND EAST

On the edge of the West End, immediately outside the City, the two districts of Holborn and Clerkenwell are often associated in name yet divided by vocation, as the former belongs to the world of law and the latter to that of the media. Their development dates back to the period of the Reformation, when the mansions of the aristocracy started to appear on the land confiscated from the Church, followed by the modern townhouses of the bourgeoisie. Today Holborn's dominant feature is the massive complex of the Inns of Court, housing the law associations, a well-proportioned arrangement of little lanes that meet in enclosed cobbled courtyards. They are gathered around Lincoln's Inn Fields, London's largest square, built in the mid-seventeenth century, along with the imposing Gothic building that houses the Royal Courts of Justice. Clerkenwell is very different and was long considered a rough district inhabited chiefly by Italian immigrants. It is the home of Little Italy, the Italian enclave bounded by Clerkenwell Road, Roseberry Avenue and Farringdon Road. The district has enjoyed a revival in recent years and has attracted small communities of artists and craftsmen with its yesteryear appearance and old streets to the north of Smithfield Market.

Beyond the elegant district of Marylebone and Regent's Park, North London comprises a wide arc from St. John's Wood in the west to Islington in the east. This area was open countryside until the mid-nineteenth century and developed with the extension of the subway line. Today these suburbs are extremely varied in type and social status. Its natural boundary with the central districts is the Regent's Canal, which skirts Regent's Park before entering the suburb of Camden. Camden is not exactly a beautiful quarter, with its jumbled mass of old factories and warehouses overlooking the canal locks and criss-crossed by railway lines and viaducts; however, it is representative of all those typically London contradictions. Its gentrification over the past 20 years has given rise to a stratified blend of rich and poor, beauty and ugliness. Today the immigrants mix with the new professionals who have recently rediscovered the district and the working-class housing contrasts with the luxury apartments along the canal designed by Nicholas Grimshaw. Camden is nonetheless loved by Londoners and tourists alike because of the enormous market that occupies much of its center along the canal, from Camden Town subway station to Chalk Farm Road.

Primrose Hill, across the railway bridge from Chalk Farm station, is a pretty village built on a hill affording a view that stretches as far as central London. Its eastern reaches, which developed around Regent's Park Road, have become a barely-out-of-town haven for a considerable number of famous people.

Like Camden, Islington has also been subjected to the process of gentrification in recent years. During the 1980s it became popular with the middle classes, who were attracted by its proximity to the City. The typical Victorian terraced houses have mostly been renovated and Upper Street has now taken on a completely new appearance, enlivened by ethnic restaurants, trendy bars and so many pub theaters as to rival the West End. Despite its revival, however, Islington remains one of London's poorest and most densely populated areas. The little districts of St. John's Wood and Little Venice, close to the Regent's Canal, are completely different. The former was built by a real-estate developer with the intention of creating a quarter for the wealthy classes, with Italian-style villas and elegant terraces. The experiment seems to have been successful, judging from the famous inhabitants of the area. Little Venice is one of the City's most charming corners, with its houseboats and flower-bedecked barges that give the entire neighborhood a romantic air.

Hampstead can be described as London's "uptown" quarter. Not only is it located in an enviable position atop a hill, but it has also been one of the City's most exclusive suburbs since the times in which it was a renowned eighteenth-century spa resort. It has changed little since those days and Hampstead has preserved its character of a quiet village far from the chaotic City. Construction speculation has left the splendid Georgian and Victorian houses intact, along with the labyrinth of alleys. The streets in the center are still adorned with the plaques bearing the names of the famous people who once inhabited them, from Agatha Christie to Sigmund Freud. The main street, Heath Street, is set on a hill and the lanes

146-147 from left to right
The Millennium Dome; the residential district of Hampstead; the Greater London

Authority Building, London's new City hall designed by Norman Foster; the London 2012 Olympic Site.

148 Canary Wharf is London's second financial district after the City and has developed on the Isle of Dogs, a strip

of land along the Thames, opposite Greenwich. The area is dominated by the Canary Wharf Tower, built by Cesar Pelli.

and squares leading off it conceal the handsome old houses, which have often been converted into museums, expensive stores and literary cafés. Hampstead Heath, the most famous North London park, is an expanse of five square miles comprising the green fields of Parliament Hill, the wild woods of West Heath and the English gardens of Kenwood House. The Heath managed to escape construction—probably against its owner's wishes—and was declared a public park in 1871. It forms the boundary between Hampstead and Highgate, another distinctive village, which is particularly famous for its cemetery in which Karl Marx is buried.

In contrast to the rich West End, the "other side" of London is known as the East End. The division of the City is not merely geographic: right from its beginnings in Victorian times this district has been synonymous with poverty and degradation and its architecture marked by slums inhabited by factory workers, immigrants and sometimes even criminals. Before this time Spitalfields, Whitechapel and Hackney were quiet country villages, where the residences of the aristocracy and merchants were interspersed with small industrial works. Bricks were manufactured in Brick Lane, the bells for most of London's churches were produced at the Whitechapel Bell Foundry—that still exists today, numerous inns for visiting merchants lined Whitechapel High Street and flourishing textile and mechanical industries were in Spitalfields and Bethnal Green. As the City encroached on their territories, the villages were transformed into working-class suburbs, initially absorbing migrant flows of Jews from Eastern Europe and more recently, refugees from Bangladesh. Over the years the Georgian and Victorian houses have been demolished and replaced with public housing. Today the districts of the East End are experiencing a true revival following a long period of decline. Spitalfields, whose center is marked by Christ Church, is a lively blend of fashionable locales and kitsch Indian shops and restaurants, especially around Brick Lane, the main street of what has become known as Banglatown due to its large Bangladeshi community. Spitalfields Market, in the center of the district, is one of the area's rare examples of Victorian architecture, a red-brick and green-gabled hall built in 1893. The Whitechapel Art Gallery, at the beginning of Whitechapel High Street, has acted as a magnet for the new wave of artists that

has colonized the lofts of the district, converting them into galleries. The passage from rough area to "alternative" ghetto was brief and the new construction sites and numerous locales that have opened in the districts of Shoreditch and Hoxton seem to indicate that development has only just begun. The Docklands were London's old harbor area. It was Elizabeth I who ordered the construction of the docks to ensure that goods were only unloaded in the proper places. During the nineteenth century enormous quays occupied the northern bank of the river: the London Docks for coffee, fruit and cocoa; St. Katharine's Docks for sugar and rum; the West India Docks for rum and mahogany; and finally the Royal Docks for all the goods from the colonies. Cubbit Town, on the Isle of Dogs, was built to provide housing for the dockers and workers of the nearby industries.

The Docklands district is the last frontier of urban development. Sandwiched between Tower Bridge and the Greenwich Peninsula, the revival of this 12-mile strip of land began in the Eighties, and for many it represents the architectural incarnation of Thatcherism. Its emblem is the Canary Wharf Tower, the 800-foot stainless-steel-clad skyscraper designed by Cesar Pelli, which towers like an obelisk over the modern buildings on the Isle of Dogs, where a bend in the Thames creates a horseshoe-shaped loop. However, the most spectacular building in the heart of the new Docklands is not representative of the area. The rest of the district is a desolate expanse of expensive lofts, old warehouses still awaiting conversion, public housing developments and anonymous skyscrapers that are constantly being joined by new buildings that often remain empty, the best example of which is the Millennium Dome. This spectacular construction, chosen as the British symbol of the new Millennium, can be seen in the distance, before Greenwich. Following the initial enthusiasm, it is now awaiting new tenants.

However, the regeneration process has only just begun. The Royal Victoria Docks will be the site of a new international exhibition center, while the Royal Albert Docks, further east, already house a Regatta Center. Wapping, the westernmost district, has retained its Victorian architecture, with old brick warehouses converted into original (and expensive) apartments. The exclusive St. Katharine Docks, the first to be renovated, has swing bridges and a quay where luxury yachts are moored.

150-151
The Millennium Dome was perhaps the building that aroused most interest on occasion of the new millennium. It was built in Greenwich to celebrate the advent of 2000 and

consists of a dome with a circumference of over half a mile, which is able to accommodate up to 10,000 people. The structure was closed at the end of 2000, as intended, and its future is still uncertain.

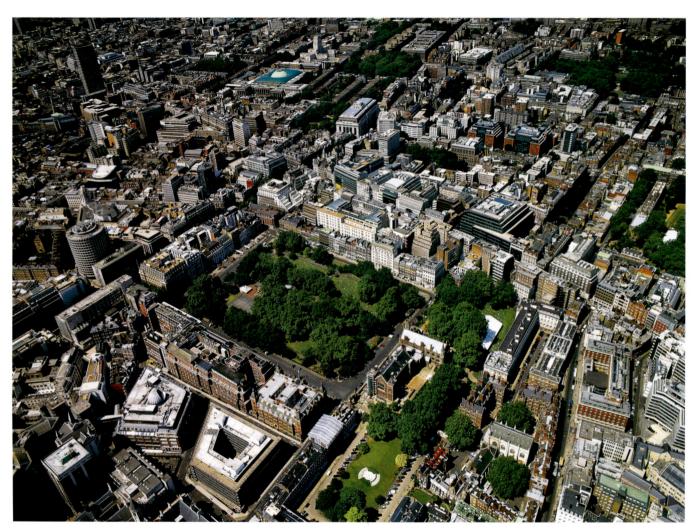

152 Lincoln's Inn, in Chancery Lane, is one of the four Inns of Court, the professional legal societies whose origins date back to the eleventh century. Each is headed by an elder member (bencher), who admits the students to the "railing" (bar), thus enabling them to

practice the profession. This is where the term "barrister" comes from.

153 London's Law Courts are also known as the Royal Courts of Justice. They are housed in an extensive building constructed

between 1874 and 1882 in a style known as Perpendicular, or Perpendicular Gothic, due to its vertical structural emphasis. The style dates back to the fourteenth century.

154-155 Lincoln's Inn Fields is the

name of the park situated in front of the premises belonging to the legal society of the same name. It was designed by Inigo Jones in the seventeenth century and covers an area of 12 acres, making it one of the City's largest squares.

156 and 157
Hampstead has
managed to retain its
appearance of a
characteristic hill
village. Sufficiently
distant from the City,
the district was an
elegant residential
and leisure area up
until the eighteenth
century. It is dotted
with groups of
houses that were
built between the
late eighteenth and
early nineteenth
centuries, later
flanked by
Victorian buildings.

158 top The buildings that constitute Smithfield Meat Market occupy an area of over seven acres and are equipped with 15 miles of tracks for hanging the sides of meat. The market is situated above an underground maze of tunnels that were once used to lead animals to the slaughterhouse, but now serve as parking or storage areas.

158-159 Smithfield Meat Market is the only remaining wholesale food market in the City, right in the center of London. This old covered market was built between 1851 and 1866, on the site of the previous livestock market.

159 The huge steel and glass tower known as the British Telecom Tower was built in 1965 for the installation of the City's telecommunications system. It is 620 feet tall and was the highest building in Britain at the time of its construction.

160 The Barbican Arts and Conference Centre was inaugurated in 1982 in the futuristic complex in the heart of the City known as the Barbican. This building has six floors, five of which are below ground level, and houses an art gallery, library, theater and halls for concerts and conferences. It is surrounded by three reinforced concrete residential towers.

160-161 Broadgate was built in 1985 on the site of the old Broad Street Station. The complex is composed of 39 buildings arranged around squares and gardens. Its center is the Arena, in Broadgate Square, which hosts various events.

162 top left and 163 The enormous glass and steel hemisphere overlooking the southern bank of the Thames is London's new City Hall. The building was designed by Norman Foster to house the Greater London Authority, the City's local government. City Hall's 10 stories provide a total area of 183,000 square feet of floor space that houses all the administrative departments of the Greater London Authority, public services, the mayor's offices and the Council Chamber, all enclosed in an enormous glass shell.

162 top right A competition was held for the construction of the new City Hall, not only to find the best building, but also the best location. An evocative site on the south bank of the Thames near Tower Bridge was chosen, situated at the center of an area currently undergoing exciting social and architectural transformation.

162 bottom The illustrious HMS Belfast is today moored on the south bank of the Thames, near Tower Bridge. The ship was used by the Royal Navy during World War II and up until 1965.

164 The little Isle of Dogs peninsula has gone from being the heart of the Docklands to a mass of modern skyscrapers. It can be reached only by the river or the Docklands Light Railway, which connects the area to the City.

165 The 2012 Summer Olympic Games prompted a redevelopment of many of the areas of London. The Olympic Stadium – the centerpiece of the 2012 Summer Games – is located at Marshgate Lane in Stratford in the Lower Lea Valley.

166-167 The Docklands comprise the wharves to the north and south of the Thames. The entire area is characterized by old warehouses and industrial architecture that has now been partly restored or converted into modern apartments and offices.

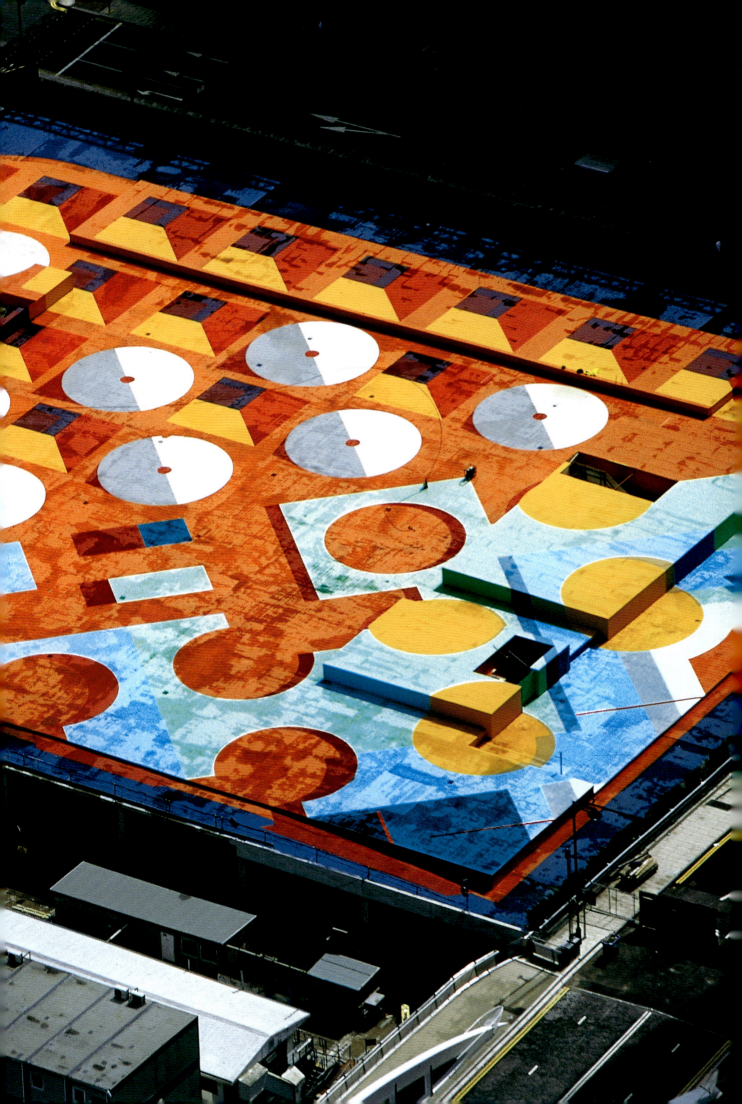

SOUTH

OF THE RIVER

The historical town of Greenwich is London's southeastern gateway. Although just a half-hour subway ride from the City center, Greenwich's atmosphere of a picturesque village on the river actually makes it a world apart. The town is home to an extraordinary complex of buildings by leading British architects, which have made it a UNESCO World Heritage site. What visitors see today was constructed gradually over the centuries, as Greenwich became the residence of various English kings. However, the most significant historical time for the town was the Tudor period. The first palace to be built was Bella Court, overlooking the river and commissioned by the brother of Henry V. The huge surrounding estate was enclosed a few years later, creating Greenwich Park, the largest in London, with wide avenues, a deer reserve and rose gardens. It was designed by the French landscape gardener Le Nôtre, who was also responsible for the gardens of Versailles. Greenwich was altered extensively during the reign of Queen Anne and now has a more classical style. In 1611, Inigo Jones built the Queen's House, the first English Renaissance building, which was later extended by Jones's nephew, John Webb. The complex assumed its current appearance with Christopher Wren. The four perfectly symmetrical palaces of the Old Royal Naval College were built facing each other, leaving the Queen's House as a central landmark, at the end of an ideal walk offering a magnificent view over the Thames. Right next to it is a large building with a spectacular glass roof that houses the Maritime Museum. Beyond this extraordinary architectural complex, Greenwich is a small town with handsome terraces built around open squares, enlivened by cafés, bookstores, antique stores and—on weekends—antique and craft markets. The Old Royal Observatory, located on the highest hill of Greenwich Park, enjoys superb views over the rest of London.

Until recently Brixton was just a suburban corner of Greater London, an expanse of typical red-brick terraced houses crisscrossed by ugly viaducts. It was colonized during Victorian times, with the arrival of the railway, and following the Second World War became the City's West Indian quarter, the scene of riots during the 1990s. In short, Brixton has never been one of the trendiest residential districts, yet today it is certainly among the most fascinating and lively areas of the City. Its center is characterized by Brixton Market, a huge market symbolizing the neighborhood's multicultural variety. The stalls stretch out beyond Electric Avenue, one of the first shopping streets in the City to have been lit with electric lamps, before invading the covered arches of Granville Arcade and continuing as far as Brixton Road. The Brixton Windmill, at the far end of Blenheim Gardens, is a pleasant surprise in the urban wilderness of this part of London; it was built in 1816 and its sails are still intact. Slightly further east, Brockwell Park is the district's green lung, and it has a 1930s lido and a garden atop a hill affording beautiful views over London. Just a few miles away is Dulwich, a village that looks as if it got there by accident. The neighborhood is isolated by parks and gardens and grew up around the spa of Dulwich Wells. It has preserved its appearance of a country village, with pretty Georgian houses, stores with a vintage air and even a few old cottages.

168-169 from left to right Hampton Court Palace, surrounded by Hampton Court and Bushy Parks; the suburb of Brixton; the Old Royal Naval College in Greenwich; the loop in the Thames at Greenwich opposite the Old Royal Naval College.

171 Hampton Court Palace was founded in the twelfth century as a royal residence and rearranged over the following 500 years. Its sheer size enables visitors to choose between six different themed itineraries.

The southern bank of the Thames has found a new lease of life. This was once a district of bad repute, outside the jurisdiction of the City and dedicated to the quest for prohibited pleasures, ranging from taverns to Elizabethan theaters and brothels. Today Southbank and Southwark are once again two of the most exciting quarters of London, although in different ways, becoming centers of leisure and cultural magnets. The rediscovery of the area over the past decade has turned it into fertile ground for City planning experiments, recovering obsolete and abandoned spaces that have been added to the existing institutions such as the South Bank Center, National Theatre and Design Museum. Bankside Power Station, a splendid example of industrial architecture built from red bricks, has been converted into the Tate Modern, the section of the famous gallery dedicated to modern and contemporary art. In this area of the City the skyline has been altered by the signs of the architectural frenzy to celebrate the Millennium in 2000, leaving a legacy of new modernity: the 450-foot British Airways London Eye ferris wheel, the Millennium Mile pedestrian walk and the Millennium Bridge, the narrow pedestrian bridge across the Thames that connects its south bank to the Cathedral and the City. New museums have sprung up, the old theater where Shakespeare's plays were staged has been rebuilt and fashionable locales have appeared. As a result, Londoners have rediscovered this area between Tower Bridge and the new ultramodern Waterloo Station, a well-proportioned blend of modern and contemporary architecture and the romantic corners of the City of the past.

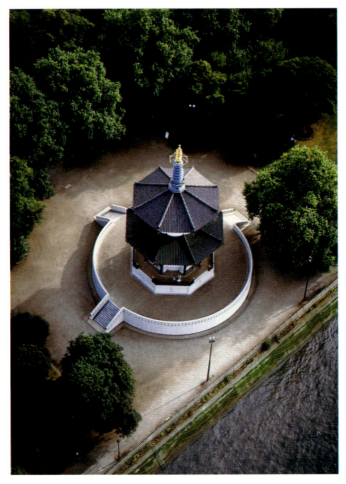

172 Hyde Park and Kensington Gardens are urban parks on a human scale, embellished with furnishings in various architectural styles.

173 A trip on the London Eye, on the South Bank, is an unusual way of admiring a panoramic view of the whole of London. The view from the top of the wheel reaches over 25 miles, as far as Windsor Castle.

West London commences where the Thames turns south. From Chiswick to Hampton the course of the river is marked by villages with handsome country estates that have lost nothing of their rural character, despite having been swallowed up by the City. In the eighteenth century the district was already a well-known holiday area for the aristocratic Londoners who had built their country houses there. This suburban region is characterized by its greenery: Wimbledon Common and Putney Heath merge to form London's largest public green area, whereas Richmond Park is the largest royal park and one of the country's most important nature reserves. The Royal Botanic Gardens at Kew, on the bank of the Thames, are like a veritable "green" museum. However, the area has even more oases. A succession of country and stately homes run from Chiswick to Osterley, from the Palladian Chiswick House to the better-known Syon House, one of the most significant works of the Georgian architect Robert Adam. Syon House, three miles from Osterley Park, is a house that gives the impression of being set in open country. What was once a flat and even plot was improved with the addition of imaginative landscaped gardens and a lake. Ham House, in Twickenham, is a seventeenth-century building with its original gardens; and Hogarth's House, which belonged to the famous English painter, also dates back to the same period.

The Royal Botanic Gardens at Kew are undoubtedly among London's most famous gardens. They were founded in 1759 and grew to comprise 120 acres of lawns with 50,000 species of plants protected by ornamental Victorian greenhouses, such as the marvelous mid-nineteenth century wrought-iron and glass Palm House. However, the most unusual building in the grounds is the ten-floor Chinese pagoda, which bears witness to the eccentricity and creativity of these gardens that were first created as part of a royal estate. During the middle of the nineteenth century, when Kew Gardens had already been donated to the nation, the landscape gardener of Regent's Park, W.A. Nesfield, added the magnificent vistas and designed the lake and pond.

Richmond is a town of gardens and old houses on the banks of the Thames. Riverside, the pedestrian area along the Thames, is a complex of fairly recently terraced houses that perfectly imitate the classic style. Riverside offers views of London's oldest surviving bridge, the five-span stone Richmond Bridge, built in 1777. Other elegant seventeenth- and eighteenth-century buildings are built round Richmond Green, one of London's most beautiful parks. Higher up, Richmond Hill, with its steep terraces reaching down to the river, is a splendid vantage point for viewing the Thames Valley, London and the neighboring counties. The area actually holds a record in terms of green spaces: Richmond Park, whose 2,500 acres of woodland and fields unfold below the hill, is Europe's largest urban park, which has been left in a practically natural state.

Hampton Court Palace, the most handsome royal residence, is an enormous red-brick complex overlooking the Thames. It was built as an ecclesiastic palace before becoming the property of Henry VIII, who further embellished the already sumptuous building. It was rearranged by Christopher Wren during the second half of the seventeenth century, with the intention of turning it into an English version of Versailles, but his work was limited to the reconstruction of the south and east wings and the addition of the Banqueting House. It is surrounded by many beautiful gardens, ornamental lakes, a vineyard and the indoor tennis court created by Henry VIII. The Maze, to the north of the Palace, is what remains of the original four hedge mazes that were created in 1714. Pilgrims would crawl through them on their hands and knees as a sort of penitence. Bushy Park extends beyond the Lion Gates, the majestic entrance gates to the palace, is another park designed by Wren: it is an almost wild reserve where red and fallow deer run free.

175 The riverside complex of the Old Royal Naval College in Greenwich is composed of several structures: the Queen's House with the National Maritime Museum (center) is perfectly framed by the four buildings that form the Old Royal Naval College.

176 Once inside the
main gate, Hampton
Court Palace is
entered through
the Great House
(foreground), which
is flanked by two
wings built during
the reign of Henry
VIII, as
commemorated by
the coats of arms
that decorate the
central loggia.

177 Hampton
Court Palace stands
on the northern
bank of the
Thames, upstream
of the City, and is
surrounded by the
huge Hampton
Court and Bushy
Parks. It also
boasts numerous
Tudor, Baroque
and Victorian
gardens.

178 London has the worst traffic congestion problems in the whole of Britain and some of the worst in Europe. The City's network of public buses is one of the most extensive in the world: each day over 6,500 buses transport approximately five million passengers on 700 different lines.

179 The southern part of London is composed of a tangle of formerly shabby suburbs, such as Brixton. Today this typical Victorian district with its brick houses has become one of the liveliest in the City, with a colorful market and a large Afro-Caribbean community.

180-181 Around 1,700 tons of steel were used to build the London Eye. The huge wheel exceeds the weight of 250 of the City's traditional red double-decker buses.

182 The Tate Modern was inaugurated in 2000 in the former Bankside Power Station and is the focus of the new cultural leisure center south of the Thames. In addition to its collection of international modern art, the huge building houses four restaurants and an auditorium. The top floor offers breathtaking views over the opposite side of the river.

183 The new Globe Theatre stands on the south bank of the Thames on the same site as the original theater, which was built in 1599 and subsequently destroyed. The current building is the result of a campaign spearheaded in 1970 by American actor Sam Wanamaker and finally inaugurated in 1997.

*184 The Royal Chelsea
Hospital was inspired
by Les Invalides in Paris
and the building was
commissioned to
Christopher Wren by
Charles II and intended
to house 500 war
veterans.*

*185 top London has
recently witnessed a
new building boom,
which has renewed
the industrial area
of Southwark,
transforming it into
a residential and
cultural magnet.*

*185 bottom
The results of the
City's latest
architectural
experiments can be
seen in Southwark,
where the old
industrial structures*

*have been renovated
and new buildings
have appeared.*

*186-187 Waterloo
is Britain's largest
railway station.
In 1993 it was*

*extended with the
International
Terminal for the
Eurostar trains that
pass beneath the
English Channel to
connect London and
Paris.*

189 top Although Greenwich is part of Greater London, it is a pretty little town in its own right, set in the greenery. It is known throughout the world for its "0 Meridian" and is still home to the old Royal Observatory, which stands on top of a hill dominating a park that slopes down towards the river.

190-191 The modern Thames Barrier was built in 1974 and inaugurated ten years later. It is composed of nine reinforced concrete bridges surmounted by steel gates, which form six wide passages for boats and four narrower ones.

188 top The Greenwich Foot Tunnel is a pedestrian underpass beneath the Thames that connects the Cutty Sark Garden in Greenwich to the Isle of Dogs, a sort of "island" created by a loop in the river, which offers a splendid view of the Old Royal Naval College.

188 bottom The Cutty Sark is now housed in a garden overlooking the Thames and is the last testimony of the period of greatest splendor of British trade with the East. The old tea clipper was built in Scotland in 1869.

188-189 The Old Royal Naval College is built on the site where Greenwich Palace once stood. It is a UNESCO World Heritage Site and is composed of four separate buildings, each of which has its own inner courtyard.

192 *The Queen
Victoria Memorial
faces Buckingham
Palace. It was made
with white marble
in 1911 by the*
*sculptor Thomas
Brock and the
architect Aston
Webb. Above, on the
pinnacle, is a gilded
figure of Victory.*